KU-386-400

Myra Shackley

Wildlife tourism

INTERNATIONAL THOMSON BUSINESS PRESS
I ⓣ P An International Thomson Publishing Company

London • Bonn • Boston • Johannesburg • Madrid • Melbourne • Mexico City • New York • Paris
Singapore • Tokyo • Toronto • Albany, NY • Belmont, CA • Cincinnati, OH • Detroit, MI

Wildlife tourism

First published 1996 by International Thomson Business Press

I ⓣ P   A division of International Thomson Publishing Inc.
The ITP logo is a trademark under licence

British Library Cataloguing-in-Publication Data
A catalogue record of this book is available from the British Library

First edition 1996

Typeset in 10/12 pt Times by Cambrian Typesetters, Frimley, Surrey
Printed in the UK by Biddles Ltd, Guildford and King's Lynn

ISBN 0–415–11539–6

International Thomson Business Press
Berkshire House
168–173 High Holborn
London WC1V 7AA
UK

International Thomson Business Press
20 Park Plaza
14th Floor
Boston MA 02116
USA

http://www.thomson.com/itbp.html

Contents

Figures

Tables

Acknowledgements

I am greatly indebted to the many friends and colleagues who contributed references, suggestions and ideas for this book and to Nottingham Trent University for supporting much of the relevant fieldwork. Specific illustrations were kindly provided by the following individuals and institutions: Australian National Parks and Wildlife Service (Figure 3.1), Cayman Islands Department of Tourism (Figure 3.2), The Province of British Columbia (Canada) (Figure 4.1), Alaska Division of Tourism (Figure 4.3), John Hunt, Scientific Exploration Society (Figure 4.5), Georgina Hamilton (Figure 6.2).

Series Editors' Foreword

The International Thompson Business Press Series in Tourism and Hospitality Management is dedicated to the publication of high quality textbooks and other volumes that will be of benefit to those engaged in tourism, hotel and hospitality education, especially at degree and postgraduate level. The series has two principal strands: core textbooks on key areas of the curriculum; and the *Topics in Tourism Hospitality* series which includes highly focused and shorter texts on particular themes and issues. All the authors in the series are experts in their own fields, actively engaged in teaching, research and consultancy in tourism and hospitality. Each book comprises an authoritative blend of subject-relevant theoretical considerations and practical applications. Furthermore, a unique quality of the series is that it is student oriented, offering accessible texts that take account of the realities of administration, management and operations in tourism and hospitality contexts, being constructively critical without losing sight of the overall goal of providing clear accounts of essential concepts, issues and techniques.

The series is committed to quality, accessibility, relevance and originality in its approach. Quality is ensured as a result of a vigorous refereeing process, unusual in the publication of textbooks. Accessibility is achieved through the use of innovative textual design techniques, and the use of discussion points, case studies and exercises within books, all geared to encouraging a comprehensive understanding of the material contained therein. Relevance and originality together result from the experience of authors as key authorities in their fields.

The tourism and hospitality industries are diverse and dynamic industries and it is the intention of the editors to reflect this diversity and dynamism by publishing quality texts that enhance topical subjects without losing sight of enduring themes. The Series Editors and Advisor are grateful to Steven Reed of International Thompson Business Press for his commitment, expertise and support of this philosophy.

Stephen J. Page   Roy C. Wood
Massey University – Albany   The Scottish Hotel School
Auckland   University of Strathclyde
New Zealand

Preface

The quality of the natural environment plays, as we all know, a primary role in attracting tourists to specific destinations. For some visitors environmental quality may actually be a determinant of demand, rather than a bonus, and this is particularly so for those 'wildlife tourists' seeking an experience which will enable them to explore, no matter for how short a time, a new ecosystem and all its inhabitants. Not all these visitors have the same motivations. Some may be seriously interested in the conservation of endangered species, the maintenance of biodiversity or scientific research in a particular habitat. Others may wish to photograph wildlife and a small minority will desire to hunt it. Some visitors are lifelong wildlife enthusiasts and others merely taking a day trip to a wilderness area from a luxury hotel base. Many such visitors seek to be informed and educated although others wish primarily to be entertained.

There are as many different kinds of wildlife-watching holiday as there are kinds of wildlife. A tourist can choose between a luxury hotel-based safari in Kenya, wilderness backpacking in the Rockies or an Antarctic cruise to watch penguins and killer whales. The financial costs of such a holiday may be very considerable but unlike other types of activity tourism the physical effort required can be minimal. Some wildlife holidays need sophisticated infrastructures such as tarred access roads and luxury accommodation. At the other extreme it is possible to take a wildlife-watching holiday virtually in one's own back yard. Alternatively, the wildlife can be kept in captivity in a variety of contexts such as zoos, circuses or aquaria for permanent exhibition to visitors.

The tourism industry will double in size during the next 10 years and seasonality will be less pronounced. The real cost of long haul travel is decreasing with the result that more and more people are able to take affordable holidays to destinations that were once the preserves of the rich and famous. A modest safari holiday in Kenya can now be obtained for little more than the cost of a medium-priced package to Spain. But what of the environmental costs? Increased interest in safari holidays means that in the more frequented parts of East Africa visitors may see more zebra-striped minibuses than zebra. Second-time visitors, if not disillusioned by their experience, seek less frequented locations and pass the problems on to the less crowded National Parks system of South Africa (where tourism is expanding at 30 per cent per year), Namibia, Botswana and Zimbabwe.

Such developments must be set against steadily increasing environmental awareness where the consumer feels confident to challenge the suppliers of products and services in the tourism industry, as in any other. Wildlife tourism may be viewed as a product to be developed and marketed and thus subject to commercial and operational pressures. Governments and tour operators generally want to reap short term economic benefits from their wildlife, often at the expense of long term sustainability. The consumer may be offered products that are ostensibly sustainable, environmentally friendly and combine the provision of a high quality experience with some tangible benefit both to wildlife and local communities, but all too often such benefits are deceptive.

A very active debate has developed involving the tourism industry and those who manage protected areas over the future of tourism development. Many (e.g. Wheeller 1991) are beginning to doubt whether much-vaunted 'soft' tourism alternatives to mass development are genuinely sustainable. The whole concept of 'ecotourism' (defined by the Ecotourism Society as 'responsible travel to natural areas which conserves the environment and improves the welfare of local people') is now under debate. Some areas which were early key players in the development of ecotourism are beginning to notice deteriorating environmental quality with increasing visitor numbers. This suggests that ecotourism impacts may eventually replicate mass tourism impacts.

However, not all wildlife tourism can be considered as ecotourism although most is non-extractive. Hunting, shooting and fishing are all leisure activities involving wildlife but they would not be considered as ecologically friendly. However, research suggests that even the best intentioned wildlife watcher produces a discernible impact on the animals and habitat that he or she is watching, with the severity of the impact being directly related to visitor numbers.

Protected areas such as National Parks or reserves are crucial in attracting wildlife tourists but few such areas are managed to the mutual benefit of all parties concerned. Successful protected area management requires co-operation between government, private sector, visitor and local people but management plans are easier to formulate than they are to implement, or to police.

Long haul and specialist tour operators have a constant need to innovate and search for new locations: threatened wildlife is a major attraction. This phenomenon, which the writer has termed the 'Galapagos Effect', dictates that the rarer the species the more likely people are to want to go and see it. This, of course, creates additional pressure on an already fragile ecosystem and may indeed be the final cause of its collapse. The eponymous Galapagos Islands themselves are a prime example but there are hundreds of others ranging from gorilla tourism in Rwanda/Zaïre to 'dragon' hunters visiting the giant lizards of Komodo in Indonesia. Even Antarctica has seen a rapid increase in tourism over the past two decades based on its natural scenery and wildlife.

Pressures on wildlife must be considered within a framework of the development of conservation and planning legislation. It is impossible to divorce the environmental impacts of tourism from the need to control population pressure and develop community involvement in resource management. Issues include the need to perceive that wild animals are earning their keep, ensuring that local communities will receive long term rewards from sustainable tourism rather than short term benefits from hunting.

There are outstanding examples of good practice in wildlife and resource management for tourism. Costa Rica, for example, has an entire and successful tourism industry based on wildlife and its National Park system, the best in Central America. More than 21 per cent of the country is protected by National Parks with a further 15 per cent in other refuges and preserves. Visitors to the country are almost exclusively motivated by the desire to see wildlife. This motivation will vary in intensity from the specialist (such as a dedicated 'twitcher') to a tourist just generally interested in animals but satisfied with a relatively superficial interaction with a species and the sense of discovery associated with that experience. This type of tourism is dependent on nature and that dependency is the basis of successful tour operations.

Doubts about the sustainability of wildlife-based tourism are complic-ated by a number of ecological issues. In many ways ecotourism is still in its infancy with the result that its precise environmental consequences are not known from experience and predictive models include substan-tial guesswork. Many of the new destination areas are incompletely studied making it difficult to determine the effects of visitors on a system whose component parts have never been recorded. Existing ecological studies are often concentrated on more visible or spectacular species; we know a lot about elephants and big cats but very little about the impact of tourism on insect and plant communities. Pressures on wildlife from tourism include habitat disturbance and alteration, population change and alteration of species balance as well as outright killing.

Very little is yet known about the tolerance levels of wildlife for human contact yet there are numerous examples of tolerance failures. How much damage can an environment take? How many people is enough? The lure of expansion is difficult to resist. This has resulted in serious conflicts between nature-based tourists and the nature that they seek. Wildlife can also manipulate visitors. There are recorded cases of hyenas in the Serengeti using stationary minibuses as a means of locating and robbing cheetah families of their prey. We are familiar with alterations to wildlife behaviour: the famous 'bearjams' of Yellowstone which result from bears bartering photo-opportunities for food and the more serious grizzly bear attacks on visitors in Canadian parks. A minor manufacturing industry has grown up to provide visitors with bearproof rubbish bins and containers. Entire communities in the developed world can also be supported by wildlife tourism. The town of Churchill in northern Manitoba is now the world capital for watching polar bears which constitutes its major economic activity, apart from some diversification into beluga whale watching in the summer months.

Issues connected with wildlife are emotive; whale watching, generally seen as non-intrusive, may actually cause severe pressure on whale communities. The decline in fishing in Newfoundland and eastern Canada has meant that many former fishing boats have converted to take visitors whale watching, not always observing the strict legal guidelines against whale harassment. Lahaina (Hawaii) and Baja (California) are host to hundreds of thousands of people a year watching migrations of grey and humpback whales. This is obviously harmless when done from the shore but work further north in Alaskan waters suggests that the sheer concentration of boats disrupts feeding and breeding behaviour. Even the placid manatees (sea cows) off the coastal waters of Florida are rapidly becoming extinct because of a growth in watersports. Studies suggest that in high season there are more divers than manatees in certain popular areas, ignoring legal guidelines in the quest for contact with a threatened species.

Most, but not all, wildlife-based tourism takes place in developing countries where the benefits are seen as employment creation, attraction of foreign exchange and the improvement of infrastructures. It is very tempting to consider short term advantage at the expense of long term sustainability. Countries with particularly severe environmental problems such as Nepal sometimes change policies to reduce impact. This is often done by controlling visitor impacts while maximising revenue and advertising pro-conservation activities such as the elephant-back safaris of Chitwan National Park or the praiseworthy Annapurna Conservation Area. New areas of the world are constantly being opened up by political change, like the formerly inaccessible Kamchatka peninsula, home to a unique fauna. Even within the developed world wilderness areas such as our own National Park system are constantly under siege from overuse but matters are improving. Wildlife tour operators are increasingly becoming experts in their destinations and host countries are conveying tourism policies to operators and controlling capacity. Much research is being carried out to establish the psychological, physical and ecological carrying capacities of destination areas and there are many examples of successful resource management zoning which can reconcile such diverse recreational activities as wildlife photography and competitive trailbike riding within one management scheme.

The growth of interest in tourism management training to solve these problems can be gauged from the proliferation of tourism education courses in the UK alone. A decade ago only two institutions in the UK offered undergraduate degrees in tourism with an annual intake of 100 students. Today, the number of single or joint subject degrees has risen to 23 with an annual intake of about 1500 students. Seventeen postgraduate courses contribute an additional 350 students. Although there is at present no consensus on a syllabus recommendations exist for a minimum core curriculum which will include seven subject areas including the significance and impact (economic, sociocultural and environmental) of tourism and issues of sustainable development. An extensive literature already exists dealing with descriptions of the industry and its operations, management and marketing (e.g. Foster 1985). Most books within this field contain one or two impact-related chapters, useful as an introduction (Gunn 1988, Lea 1988, Mill and Morrison 1985). More specialised material is also available which considers spatial developments and interactions at local, national and international scales (e.g. Ryan 1992, Theobald 1993). A third category of literature deals specifically with the economic, social, political, cultural and environmental repercussions of tourism development but until recently this has been surprisingly sparse (Murphy 1985, Pearce 1987, 1989) and mainly written for geographers. The only major available reviews of environmental impacts were those of Mathieson and Wall (1982) and Edington and Edington (1986) which constituted the classic works on the subject, though both are now rather out of date. Such broad overviews did not enable detailed discussion of individual cases which students had to retrieve from a wide variety of local, regional and national sources which could include obscure NGOs, regional tourist boards and local management plans. The formation of the Ecotourism Society in Vermont, USA, has had a very beneficial effect on the literature. Not only have they published an excellent series of textbooks, manuals and case studies (e.g. Boo 1990, Lindberg and Hawkins 1993) but their regular newsletter contains many topical items with further references to detailed published material and fieldwork. Major tourism journals such as the *Journal of Travel Research*, *Tourism Management* and *Annals of Tourism Research* often include wildlife-based case studies (such as Farrell and Runyan 1991) and supplementary material is published in environmental journals including *Geography* and the *Journal of Environmental Management*. Other significant resources include the publications of the World Tourism Organisation (e.g. Inskeep 1991, WTO 1983) and the extensive series of books and specialised studies of protected area and wilderness management from the World Conservation Monitoring Centre in Cambridge (e.g. Salm and Clark 1984).

About this book

A major difficulty with writing this book has been to separate issues which deal specifically with animals from those which are concerned with the whole range of tourism impact issues or with the arguments surrounding ecotourism or development politics. Wildlife tourism is now very big business indeed and predicted to increase dramatically over the next decade. However, its very success threatens to destroy the resources on which it depends. Strictly speaking the term 'wildlife' includes both the faunal and floral components of an ecosystem although popular usage restricts it to the former, the sense in which it has been used here.

This book tries to present examples of good and bad practice and a balanced discussion of the issues and interests at stake. Within each chapter the reader will find some case studies highlighting particular issues. The book is not intended to be an in-depth study of conservation policies, nor a sourcebook for ecotourism or a detailed work on the pros and cons of management policies for protected areas. It is intended to introduce the reader to a wide range of issues and ideas connected with tourism and wildlife management, and perhaps (incidentally) to raise some doubts about whether we can ever achieve the ideal of low impact, high value tourism or be for ever guilty of loving nature to death.

Myra Shackley

1
Introduction

'Wildlife' is a term which technically encompasses both the faunal and floral components of a natural environment. However, it is often used to refer just to fauna and this is the sense utilised here. In the Preface we have already considered some of the salient points which provide background to a study of wildlife-based tourism. Some of these relate to the dynamic development of the tourism industry, some to changing contemporary attitudes, ethics and aspirations and still others to a search for sustainable solutions to the ever-increasing problems presented by mass tourism. We can summarise these as follows by considering that the four most important background factors governing the development of wildlife tourism are:

- overall growth and product diversification in world tourism
- the development of cheaper and faster access to new destination areas
- increased levels of 'green' awareness
- the search for sustainable alternatives to mass tourism

Additionally, it is necessary to consider the effect of education and the mass media on the development of new wildlife tourism destinations. The marketing of tourism has become increasingly sophisticated and can create an enormous demand for a particular destination placing sudden and potentially catastrophic pressure upon its wildlife. This marketing need not originate from the travel industry – some of the most successful destination marketing originates in wildlife films. Their outstanding photography and high quality commentaries create a very positive image of place which stimulates popular interest in remote and fragile destinations such as Antarctica (p. 45). Not for nothing has David Attenborough been described as the wildlife tourism industry's best friend.

Growth and diversification in tourism

As we all know tourism is now the world's leading industry with an annual global turnover estimated to exceed US$ 3 trillion, a figure which will more than double to US$ 7.9 trillion by 2005 (WTO 1993). It is also the world's largest employer; the World Travel and Tourism Organisation estimates that there are now some 204 million people employed directly or indirectly by the tourism industry, nearly a quarter of the world's working population. By 1994 the tourism industry also accounted for a staggering US$ 693 billion of investment in new facilities, development and equipment, with the result that there is no longer any industry or country in the world where the impact of the tourism industry, for good or bad, has not yet been felt.

This dramatic growth in tourism as a leisure activity really started in the 1960s as the result of a complex of factors ranging from increasing middle-class affluence in western countries to the development of jumbo jets and the charter tour. Since the late 1960s and 1970s tourism's steady growth has continued except for a period of stagnation in the early 1980s. Of all the aspects of this rapid development long haul travel (with flight times over five hours) has been the most significant, stimulated by cheaper flights and increased leisure time (Smith and Jenner 1989, Frechtling 1987). Wildlife tourism has also been stimulated by the fact that today's well-educated consumers have the benefit of extensive destination advertising, readily available travel literature and a network of people to contribute word of mouth information. Taking a summer holiday watching elephants in Kenya is no longer seen either as unusual or as the type of activity that only wealthy upper-class people can afford. A substantial number of modern experienced travellers are continually searching for new and exotic destinations, their tastes and interests formed by several decades of foreign travel. As people in the industrialised world are living longer the segments of the population who have sufficient leisure time and adequate funds for overseas travel are continually increasing in size. Because of the expense involved wildlife watching, at least in developing world destinations, is not primarily a young person's holiday. Adventure travel companies such as the UK-based Exodus who offer many wildlife-based holidays report the average age of their travellers as 42. Two weeks off the beaten track in Central America or India's National Parks can easily cost in excess of £3000 per person. We can summarise this by saying that the development of wildlife tourism products and new destination areas is related to:

- ease of transport
- infrastructure and access
- political stability
- existence of wide species range or 'flagship' endangered species
- government and private sector policies.

The development of new wildlife tourism products ultimately depends on the capabilities and aspirations of individual tour operators, working in an extremely competitive market with slim profit margins. However, the range of products is now so great that it includes basic, affordable holidays at one end of the spectrum and very high quality exclusive experiences at the less price sensitive end of the market. Tour operators, and the ground handlers who deal with customers in destination areas, are usually governed by the need to make a profit and increase repeat business. This may be better achieved by maximising the quality of the visitor experience at the expense of environmental impact which may manifest itself in several ways:

- ignoring environmental impact regulations to generate additional income
- low wages and few employment opportunities for local people
- economising on training and information provision
- economic leakages
- not sharing benefits with local communities.

An example of this, discussed below (p. 65) occurs in the National Parks of East Africa where tour operators will take vehicles off the beaten track to enable passengers to see some rare species, despite the cost to the environment. This can, of course, mean that such wildlife tourism will not be sustainable in the future.

International tour operators use local ground handlers to organise their tours at destination level. They will favour ground handlers who are reliable, efficient and (most importantly) price competitive meaning that wages may be kept low and local people have few opportunities for career advancement. Although many wildlife tourists are motivated by serious interest in conservation few companies, except the best and well financed, can afford to include educational material in their packages. The consumer therefore has little information on which to base a judgement of the extent of their impact on a local ecosystem. The best ground handlers have realised that customer satisfaction depends as much on the quality of their staff as on the quality of the attraction that they are visiting. Investment in staff training is therefore not money wasted. Indeed, the commonest causes for complaints in wildlife tours are a lack of information and/or poorly trained staff. Tour operators and ground handlers who have addressed this problem can gain market share at the expense of cheaper competitors but only at the top end of the market (Kelly 1989, Krippendorf 1987).

Wildlife tourism actually depends on the quality of ground handling operations. No matter how slick the marketing or how glossy the brochure it is the visitor experience at the destination which really counts. In most developing countries ground handling companies have traditionally been expatriate owned, with consequent economic leakage (Sinclair 1992). Many operate on a shoestring and have been hampered by lack of access to capital, seasonal fluctuations in revenue and difficulties with infrastructure. A local company may not necessarily have a greater interest in conservation than an international tour operator but may be motivated by the need to create and sustain employment. Wildlife may be seen as a means to create wealth in the short term (e.g. by maximising tips from customers) without genuine concern for long term issues. However, it is easy for western customers to moralise when they have the disposable income to enjoy such vacations. Nor, as we shall see, do local communities necessarily benefit much from wildlife-based tourism unless some revenue-sharing scheme is in operation (see p. 93). Because of these problems ground handlers may go out of business very quickly and many tour operators will not guarantee utilising specific ground handling operations. Moreover, because of the lead time between carrying out the fieldwork to develop a new tour and publicising the tour in a brochure a destination area can completely change in that time. Several tour operators are currently offering tiger-watching wildlife tours to some Indian parks (such as the Manas Reserve in Assam) where no tigers are currently found. Political instability in developing countries can also mean that a tour operator is faced with the fact that certain countries have become inaccessible and pre-arranged tours must be cancelled with disgruntled passengers being offered alternative arrangements. Fortunately, the opposite process is also at work and new destinations are constantly coming on stream. A decade ago few operators featured Uganda or Tanzania, for example, whereas today both feature prominently in African wildlife-watching programmes.

New destination areas and products

Tour operators have a constant need to develop new and innovative products to satisfy the demands of increasingly sophisticated and well-educated consumers (Ingram and Durst 1989). Inevitably, many of these new destination areas are in the developing world. Such wildlife tourism projects involve co-operation between the private sector, NGOs and government departments. In general access to major national attractions (parks, forests, marine areas, waterfalls, etc.) will be government controlled with access allowed to sites for profit-making tours. The economic engine behind ecotourism development is largely in the hands of the commercial sector (hoteliers, airlines, travel agents, etc.) but economic success ultimately depends on government policies. An area will not attract visitors if it is not adequately maintained or has inadequate infrastructure. Successful public–private sector partnerships have been formed (as in the case of the private game reserves within the Kruger National Park, South Africa) but tension is the more usual result. Take the case of Namibia which has a flourishing wildlife tourism industry. The extensive Namibian National Parks system comes under the control of the Ministry of Wildlife Conservation and Tourism which is systematically being starved of capital funds. Visitor revenues received from (inadequate) entrance fees are not returned to park management which is therefore unable to maintain park accommodation to the high standard required by affluent western visitors. The result has been that private companies are building high quality visitor accommodation outside major parks such as Etosha, in the north of the country. Western tourists can stay at these lodges and be taken into the park on a daily basis. Potential visitor revenue is thus further reduced and the downward spiral is maintained. Market share is also being lost to privately owned game ranches which provide a higher quality of visitor experience and better facilities. The result will be that the run-down parks will produce diminishing visitor revenues and less money for wildlife conservation and management projects (Shackley 1993).

Although the contribution of tourism revenue to developing nations was estimated at US$ 55 million in 1988 it is very difficult to make a precise estimate of the amount which derives specifically from wildlife tourism (Lillywhite and Lillywhite 1991, Lindberg 1991). Tourist money that remains in the destination country and at the site of the visitor attraction will be of direct economic benefit to local communities. However, it is the exception rather than the rule. In most nature-based tourism the visitor buys an inclusive package from a tour operator which is pre-paid in the country of origin. The main exceptions to this are locally purchased tours bought from ground handlers by budget or business travellers already in the area. Most of the costs of a package are occasioned by the airfare, accommodation and meals. On-site expenditure includes meals and the wages of local porters and guides together with local transportation and entrance fees (although these may also be paid in advance). A World Bank study claimed that 55 per cent of gross revenues leaked back to developed countries, though this was substantially reduced for ecotourism projects (Boo 1990). Part of the reason may be that such developments sometimes have lower capital investment requirements (perhaps by using local materials). Revenues received by the government (public sector) include tourist taxes, airport taxes and entrance fees to parks plus donation fees and any profit from the sale of guidebooks and souvenirs bought in National Parks. Tourism can also produce revenue from donations. The Darwin Research Institute in the Galapagos raised US$150 000 through a direct mail appeal to visitors who had signed its guest book. The Monteverde Cloud Forest Reserve in Costa Rica was financed entirely by donations to a conservation league. In theory public sector revenue will contribute to a general fund, out of which comes money to finance specific parks and conservation projects. Direct private sector revenue comes from transport, accommodation, catering and merchandising (Western and Henry 1979). A substantial portion of wildlife tourism benefits are lost to the country by leaks to overseas individuals and organisations. These leakages would include paying for infrastructure, importing oil and consumer goods and repatriation of profits (Cater 1992, McNeely 1988).

Tourism can come to dominate a destination country's foreign exchange earnings (in excess of 70 per cent in the case of the Bahamas, Dominican Republic, Jamaica, etc.) (Laarman and Durst 1987). Tourists coming to view wildlife may be a major source of revenue for governments. They pay visa, permit and park entry fees, spend money at concessions and buy accommodation, food and drink. Such cash can be used for managing resources or assisting local communities but all too often it disappears into general government funds and is never fully returned to conservation or community projects. Unfortunately the travel industry in the developing world often suffers from inappropriate government policies and tourism regulations, as well as undercapitalisation and a lack of credit, educational materials or adequate staff training programmes. Many governments take a very short term view (the need to generate revenue during their political life) compared with local communities or conservation research scientists whose longer time scales may cause internal tensions. Unfortunately tourism is also, in many ways, a fragile and unreliable base for the economy of a country (Butler 1980). The volume of visitors to a destination can be affected by a number of factors such as political instability. The effects of the Gulf War caused a dramatic decline in visits to East Africa whereas increased optimism about the future political stability of South Africa is having the opposite effect. The late 1980s drought in Zimbabwe also affected tourism, and countries like Rwanda, currently suffering a tragic civil war, have seen the almost complete destruction of a tourism infrastructure which once underpinned its entire economy. Neighbouring Uganda is now struggling to rebuild its once magnificent system of National Parks after their destruction under the dictator Idi Amin. All these countries have tourism industries which are based around the conservation of wildlife (Plog 1974).

Africa contains by far the most popular wildlife-watching tourism destinations. Multi-national adventure tour operators such as Exodus or Explore generally offer more tours in Africa than all other countries combined, although Central and South America (particularly Ecuador, Costa Rica and the Amazon Basin) are increasing in popularity. India, Indonesia and Indochina are also developing rapidly with destinations such as the Canadian Arctic, Iceland or The Gambia developing specialised wildlife tourism products. In Africa the best-known wildlife tourism destinations are the East African reserves such as the Masai Mara and Serengeti conservation areas which protect huge herds of game animals including (among others) 1.5 million wildebeests and 250 000 zebra. Other significant areas with smaller, more specialised, products are the Virunga Mountains of Uganda, Zaïre and Rwanda for mountain gorillas and relatively new destinations such as the Moremi Wildlife Preserve in Botswana. This has 36 species of mammals plus outstanding birdlife and includes the Okavango Delta, one of the most biologically diverse regions in the world. Access to a relatively new area such as this is helped by improvements in transport and infrastructure as well as political stability. The gaining of independence by Namibia and the cessation of internal conflicts in Zimbabwe enable tourists to combine the spectacular National Parks of Namibia, Botswana and Zimbabwe in one trip focused around the Victoria Falls. The traditional safari destinations of Kenya, now overcrowded, are losing market share to new parks in Zambia (with an estimated 191 wild mammal species) and Zimbabwe. South Africa's system of national and privately owned reserves has seen significant recent investment and increases in visitors and expensive minority-interest destinations such as Madagascar may be booked out months ahead. The situation in West Africa is less optimistic. Here special-interest tourism is still dominated by cultural and historical landscapes and there is less scope for wildlife tourism due to greater population densities and different natural ecosystems. The savanna grasslands of East Africa are still the most popular destinations but small West African countries like The Gambia have developed specialised wildlife programmes based around its diversity of birdlife (Sayer 1981). Sierra Leone had incipient wildlife tourism until recent civil war meant that much of the wildlife in one of its southern National Parks was killed and eaten by refugees. It is possible to visit the Cameroons to see lowland gorillas and the Atlas Mountains fringing the Sahara to see desert antelope but visitor numbers are still very low. Many areas of the world have vast untapped potential for wildlife-based tourism. Even in Sub-Saharan Africa, for example, only a few countries have been successful though many more have potential such as Tanzania, whose tourist lodges are currently being privatised and modernised after years of state neglect, and Uganda, currently restocking its depleted parks.

Certain speciality destinations such as Royal Chitwan National Park in Nepal or the orang-utan reserves of Indonesia and Borneo (see p. 73) are immensely popular but other Asian destinations such as the Indian National Parks which once formed part of Project Tiger (p. 77) are losing business. The fastest-growing destination areas are in Central and South America. Wildlife tourism is becoming a major motivator for Ecuador (especially the Galapagos National Park), Costa Rica and Belize. More than 75 per cent of visitors to Ecuador are motivated by an interest in wildlife, with a corresponding figure of 50–60 per cent for Belize and Costa Rica (Ankomah and Crompton 1990, Butler 1991).

Green awareness

The developed world has become more aware of 'green' issues since the 1980s, with a resulting increase not only in membership of environmental organisations but in an interest in the natural world. The search for a life-enhancing experience to be obtained by visiting some as yet undeveloped area has contributed to an annual growth rate estimated at 20 per cent for nature-based tourism in general (Snepenger 1987, Snepenger and Moore 1989). Wildlife tourism is essentially a phenomenon which appeals to citizens of the developed world in the 20th century. We have progressed beyond a philosophy which considered that species which were unable to compete with humans did not deserve to survive. That 'survival of the fittest' idea underpinned many of the hunting-based tourism activities which were to develop into today's non-destructive wildlife tourism. Today the majority of western people like the idea of sharing their planet with a diverse range of wildlife, although this basic sympathy with animals is by no means shared in poorer, less developed, countries. In the west an interest in animals may be manifest only in the keeping of a pet or stocking a birdtable but most thinking people would profess sympathy for, and empathy with, animals struggling to survive in ever-contracting environments. The green revolution of the 1980s has reinforced the view that conserving the planet means making efforts to conserve all its inhabitants as well.

Animals are often the focus of environmental conservation movements since it is easier to identify with the plight of an animal than with a total ecosystem. Many who weep over the fate of the giant panda would be quite unconcerned about the status of the bamboo on which it feeds. The extensive publicity given to the survival problems of certain species such as the panda has created environmental discrepancies in people's heads. Conservation-minded westerners also find it easier to feel sorry for a large endangered mammal than to sympathise with local people with whom that mammal is competing for food and land. It is difficult, bearing in mind the cultural gap, to imagine what life is like for underprivileged people who need to make a living from land that is occupied by wildlife. The elephant that we in the west see as a wonderful photo-opportunity is likely to be feared (and shot) by local communities whose crops it destroys.

Visitors are becoming increasingly willing to take an active interest in wildlife such as participating in conservation holidays (p. 51). This has resulted in the formation of organisations such as Earthwatch which was founded in 1971 to 'preserve fragile lands, monitor change and conserve endangered species'. Its scientific expeditions now draw around 35 000 people a year for working vacations on any one of 2000 projects throughout the world. Such programmes range from tracking timber wolves to counting humpback whales off Mozambique. The Coral Cay Conservation Programme in Belize (see p. 51) confirms that some people are willing to pay very considerable costs to spend their holidays actively participating in wildlife conservation programmes (Tabata 1989). Unfortunately, there are some cases where an ostensibly 'green' tourism company merely pays lip service to the aims of conservation by contributing cash either to environmental charities or to local community projects (Wight 1993). The amounts involved are usually small and written off against tax. The existence of such schemes makes the customer feel that he or she has contributed some kind of benefit although this may have very little effect at local, regional or national level. The process is merely a marketing device, often referred to as 'greenwashing'. These slim budgets may also mean that local needs such as training are pruned. Within protected areas such as National Parks managers frequently complain that tour operators get all the benefits from the parks but contribute nothing to their upkeep. There are some notable exceptions to this generalisation, including the company which leads birdwatching trips to Costa Rica and gives $50 per visitor to buy threatened rainforest. Another company mounted a campaign in its newsletter, sent as a mailshot to each person on its 10 000 address mailing list, pledging to contribute cash for every bird seen on a particular trip. The campaign raised $16 000 for conservation. Small companies often contribute more practical help at ground level than larger operators who sometimes make donations to international conservation groups.

Much, though far from all, wildlife tourism focuses around endangered or threatened species. It is natural that tourists wish to see rare species of animals and birds which they cannot observe at home. The fact that these species may be endangered is both an opportunity and a threat. The writer once described the governing principle as the 'Galapagos Effect', which says that the more endangered the species the more likely people are to want to visit it, thereby increasing the pressure on its environment and (ultimately) probably increasing the chances of its extinction. This may be an exceptionally pessimistic view. Most wildlife tourism programmes dealing with endangered species aim, of course, to achieve exactly the opposite and utilise tourism revenues for conservation purposes. The IUCN Red Data Book is the conservation bible identifying species at risk. It provides the basic information needed to integrate local development needs and national development priorities with conservation priorities. The World Conservation strategy produced *e du. phgra.*

by IUCN/WWF/UNEP emphasises the need for environmental education as one method for influencing people's perceptions of environmental problems. In Africa such education programmes can reduce the
impact of hunting and poaching by providing alternative sources of
revenue for local communities and stimulating the view of wildlife as a
benefit rather than a threat.)The Zimbabwe CAMPFIRE programme
(p. 93) is an excellent example of this process. However, such work is
expensive and cannot generally be funded by governments alone. This is
where wildlife tourism becomes significant at a grass-roots level.

A great deal of interest is currently focused on the ethical and moral
issues surrounding the keeping of animals in captivity. Many people
believe that it is wrong to utilise animals as part of circus or cabaret acts,
and that it is also wrong to encourage blood sports such as bullfighting
or hunting. Questions are also being raised (see p. 80) about the ethics
of sportfishing, a popular leisure activity for a substantial segment of the
population. Popular attitudes to zoos and other wildlife attractions have
altered extensively during the last decade but visiting zoos is still
popular; a recent survey indicated that more than half the UK
population had visited a zoo, wildlife or safari park over the past five
years. Such activities were particularly popular with families with
children. One of the interesting things which emerged from the survey
was an apparent difference which existed in people's minds between
their own motivations for making such a visit (generally just 'to have a
day out') and what should be the zoo's prime function (conservation).
This question is discussed in detail below (p. 116) in relation to the recent
problems experienced by London Zoo. This same survey (whose results
are summarised in Table 6.2) also confirmed a species bias. Zoo visitors
are drawn by big cats, nearly 30 per cent of visitors saying that seeing
tigers, lions and other cats were the favourites. This is particularly so
among men – did the attraction once contribute to the popularity of lion/
tiger shooting (p. 77)? Some 23 per cent of zoo visitors preferred apes
and monkeys with 12 per cent prioritising penguins and seals. Elephants
received a surprisingly low rating (9 per cent) and pandas 8 per cent,
perhaps because the latter are almost as rare in zoos as they are in the
wild.

In summary, then, increased levels of green awareness have affected
the development of wildlife tourism in the following ways:

● raised ethical questions about the keeping of animals in captivity and
extractive wildlife-based leisure activities

- considered ways of utilising tourism revenues for conservation purposes
- emphasised the plight of threatened species and the role of tourism in their survival
- enabled tour operators to develop environmentally friendly wildlife tourism products, not all of which are genuine
- stressed the need for sustainable community benefits from wildlife tourism.

The search for alternative tourism

This need for a continual supply of exotic destinations combined with the strong currencies of the developed world has meant that international tourist arrivals in developing countries have more than doubled since 1976. Global tourism is growing at 23 per cent faster than the overall world economy with more than 500 million tourists travelling each year. This will probably increase to 937 million by the year 2010 with consequent massive social, cultural and environmental damage. The gradual realisation that such adverse impacts are almost inevitable is behind the many new approaches to tourism designed to respond to a growing awareness of such problems. Terms such as

- environmentally friendly tourism
- sustainable tourism
- ecotourism
- responsible tourism
- low impact tourism

are just a few among many in common use, discussed below (Mowforth 1993). These designate low impact tourism programmes which might result in some form of sustainable benefits to the destination area (Hall and Weiler 1992). Issues which dominate the growth and sustainability of any tourism industry in the long term are inevitably related to the physical environment. Long term success rests on the ability to maintain a high environmental quality with a carefully established tourism carrying capacity and an understanding of what the environmental impacts of tourism are likely to be.

Ecotourism (a term invented by conservationists in the 1970s) is defined by the Ecotourism Society as 'responsible travel that conserves the natural environment and sustains the well-being of local people'. This definition clearly includes a spectrum of activities that do not involve watching wildlife.)As we have already seen ecotourism is often nothing more than a marketing tool.(In theory it should be an economically and socially sound means to conserve biodiversity, and also to provide revenue to improve the lives of people living in or near biologically important areas.)Ecotourism is the fastest-growing segment of an industry which is, as we have seen, growing rapidly out of control. It really constitutes a niche market for environmentally aware tourists who are interested in observing nature.(It is especially popular among government and conservation organisations because it can provide simultaneous environmental and economic benefits.)In theory it should be less likely than other forms of tourism to damage its own resource base but this is only true if such tourism is managed with great care.)A successful ecotourism project has got balanced social, economic and environmental objectives but even so it is existing within an international tourism market which is, as we have seen (p. 2), fragile and un-predictable.

Ecotourism projects should meet the following criteria. They must:

- be sustainable (defined as meeting present needs without compromising their ability to meet future needs)
- give the visitor a unique and outstanding experience
- maintain the quality of the environment.

This all sounds very admirable but in practice there are problems confronting both the development and management of ecotourism projects.(Many of these result from a lack of co-ordination between the different individuals and organisations concerned. These can include scientists and conservators, NGOs (non-governmental organisations), all the different branches of the travel industry, central and regional governments and local communities. Many NGOs, especially conservation organisations, have increased their activities in tourism which was traditionally regarded as a frivolity which got in the way of serious research. However, they have now realised that economic benefits from parks and protected areas can improve the chances of establishing a sustainable resource management strategy. Conservation groups and governments often lack knowledge about the ecotourism market (i.e. the travelling public) and the constraints under which the travel industry operates. A government can set unrealistic targets or move the goal posts, which can cause serious problems for an ecotourism operator who may be developing a new project with delicately balanced costing and a nine-month lead-in time. Governments can increase fees, limit access or make other changes which the operator may be forced to pass on to the public. It is often said that the only way to circumvent these problems is the development of partnerships but in practice different sets of vested interests may make it difficult for all pieces of the ecomanagement jigsaw to work together in public.

In addition to straightforward wildlife watching or photography other forms of ecotourism include adventure travel that requires physical stamina such as hiking, rafting, diving, etc. – activities preferably carried out in an unspoilt natural environment (Hall and Weiler 1992). Anthropologically motivated travel could also be included. The academic literature supporting the development of the subject is unfortunately low on quantitative data and analysis and high on speculation. Part of the reason for this stems from the relatively short distance that ecotourism has travelled into the product life cycle. It is still a new subject and there are few clear academic guidelines. The benefits from ecotourism are generally held to be substantial but much confusion exists about how they are to be obtained (Blangy and Nielsen 1993, Lindberg 1994, McNeely 1988). Some early ecotourism projects are now beginning to show serious flaws which have emerged as more becomes known about the long term impact of visitors. This is inevitable since visitors add a new dimension to a natural ecosystem which in itself has seldom been completely studied. Generally speaking certain elements will have been researched in detail and others will not have been researched at all. Research on the impact of humans on different ecosystems is even more patchy (Schoenfeld and Hendee 1978). There is an extensive literature, for example, on the impact of tourist vehicles on big cats in the African savanna (p. 67). These large animals are relatively easy to see, emotive and likely to produce large research grants. However, almost nothing is known about the potential effect of visitors on unexciting invertebrates in the same area.

Questions

1 What are the major sociocultural influences determining levels of consumer interest in wildlife tourism?
2 Write a case study of any one major wildlife tour operator, considering whether or not it operates sustainable environmental policies.
3 Conduct a piece of market research utilising interviews with a number

of wildlife tourists at a specific destination to determine their motivations.

4 After consulting the latest issue of the World Tourism Organisation annual statistics, select and evaluate the potential of any *one* country as a future wildlife tourism destination.

2
Tourists and wildlife
Interaction and impact

The dramatic growth of interest in nature tourism, discussed above, has inevitably increased the dangers of stressing fragile environments and endangered species by overexposure to visitors. The problem is compounded by lack of regulation and a scarcity of adequate management plans which mean that many popular areas are poorly documented by ecologists. There are very few examples of careful management plans involving the calculation of environmental and visitor carrying capacities (see below, p. 33). Such plans can be used to determine the precise level of visitation which is both permissible without creating environmental damage and sustainable from both economic and environmental perspectives (EIU 1991, Davies 1990).

The effect of wildlife tourism on wildlife is difficult to document without long term studies and is complicated by a series of additional factors including:

- differential popularity (not all animals are as popular as others and not all animals generate equal volumes of public concern)
- differential fragility (not all animals and ecosystems are equally fragile – some can absorb higher levels of disturbance from visitors than others which possess lower resistance)
- some animals may become habituated to human presence which alters elements of their behaviour sometimes to the advantage of nature tourists.

These three fundamental issues

Disturbance
Habituation
Carrying capacity

underpin any study of the effect of visitors on wildlife but they must be considered within the broad framework of systematic ecology. Potential disturbance by visitors, for example, is far from the greatest hazard threatening many animals. Throughout the world the existence of wildlife species which require undisturbed remote habitats is being imperilled by others factors such as:

- agricultural development
- urban expansion
- extractive industries such as logging or mining
- increased recreational use of wilderness areas.

This opening up of previously unfrequented areas may increase the potential for contact between humans and wildlife in ways that are generally detrimental to the latter's quality of life (Boyle and Samson 1985, Buckley and Pannell 1990). Ironically, such interactions may be actively sought by humans in order to enhance their own perceptions of harmony with the natural environment. The interaction process is both progressive and difficult to study. It is often true that serious irreversible damage to wildlife populations can occur before a problem is even recognised and once this occurs the situation is almost impossible to reverse. Interactions between humans and wildlife are usually un-scripted, meaning that they occur more or less by accident when people intrude on an animal's natural habitat. The walker who sees deer, badgers or foxes during a ramble in the British countryside is having such an unscripted interaction, which will probably greatly enhance the quality of experience of the walk. The whole point of successful wildlife tourism, of course, is to facilitate such encounters by taking the visitors to places where interesting interactions are most likely to occur (Giongo *et al.* 1994). This orchestration of encounters reaches its ultimate in the provision of food lures to attract wild animals to a particular locality, thus modifying not only the local habitat but also the behaviour of the wildlife being sought. Such procedures are quite common even within National Parks, and discussed below in relation to sites from Africa to Indonesia. Most unscripted interactions unfortunately constitute harass-ment by humans with effects varying from the creation of mild excitement among the wildlife being observed to severe stress culminating in death. Although such harassment is generally entirely accidental such encounters, unless very fleeting, will disturb some element of an animal's essential activities such as feeding or breeding behaviour (Neil *et al.* 1975). Animals usually react to such encounters by trying to get away, which may cause severe exertion or displacement from home territory. The problem is particularly acute among animal populations which may already be vulnerable because of poor nutrition, adverse weather, parasites or predation which makes them less resistant to human influence. Most harassment is quite unintentional, innocent and uninformed and often, ironically, carried out by those who see themselves as harmless users of countryside or wilderness areas. Some, however, is intentional and constitutes vandalism, only controlled by enforced regulation and peer pressure. It is also possible for animals to harass their visitors as the case study of bears in North American parks (below) amply demonstrates. Here we can see a progression from initial unscripted interactions such as incidental sightings which gave pleasure to the visitors. Visitors wishing to repeat the experience rewarded the animals with food, creating a begging cycle which resulted in such a drastic disturbance of the bears' feeding behaviour that they became a problem for the visitors. The solution, involving the enforced separation of bears from people, is a lot easier to postulate than it is to enforce in practice.

Separation of visitors from visited is just one of a range of possible solutions to the problem of negative interactions which start with better public education and increased research (Duffus and Dearden 1990). Unless we know what the effect of visitor activity will be on a particular species how are we to prevent or manage the consequences? Most solutions involve either controlling visitor activities (discussed in Chapter 3), or controlling the behaviour of the wildlife, which may include manipulation of habitat. No single solution fits every problem and, as we have already said, not all animals are equally vulnerable or equally attractive to visitors. Very little work has been done on what role wildlife watching plays in recreational value. Brown *et al.* (1980) surveyed wilderness hikers in Colorado quantifying factors contributing to their enjoyment (Figure 2.1). The hikers placed the highest psychological value on achieving a relationship with nature (3.2 out of possible 4) with high scores for wildlife values. Large and small animals scored the same (2.7) comparing favourably with exercise and outranking hiking. Would the results have been different if the survey population was families on campgrounds, hunters or birdwatchers?

	Value[a]
Psychological Attributes:	
Relationship with nature	3.2
Escape physical pressure	2.9
Exercise	2.6
Freedom	1.9
Achievement	1.6
Reflection on personal values	1.3
Wildlife Values:	
Larger wildlife (bighorn sheep, deer, mountain goats)	2.7
Small wildlife (beaver, ptarmigan, and other birds)	2.7
Good fishing	2.4
Naturally reproducing fish	2.4

Source: Brown *et al.* (1980).
[a]Scale: highest value = 4.0; no value = 0.0; strongest negative value = −4.0.

Figure 2.1 Some values obtained by cluster analysis of perceived contributions to recreational experience of backcountry hikers in the Weminuche area of Colorado

Wildlife attractiveness to visitors

A significant study by Bart (1972) established that personal likes and dislikes are culturally determined, affecting the animals' public image and thus the potential strength of feeling which might protect an endangered species. An animal with a poor public image (such as the North American timber wolf or the African brown hyena) is often portrayed maliciously on film which prejudices conservation efforts with the result that its survival is threatened by humans. In Bart's study 88 student volunteers were administered a 30-item 'animal interest' questionnaire. The results are summarised in Table 2.1. The survey gave high responses to safe, common domestic animals with low rankings and low percentages of positive responses to certain rare and endangered species such as alligator, wolf, falcon, hawk and vulture. The lowest ratings of all were given to animals which were perceived as dangerous, frightening or dirty, such as snakes, spiders or rats. This suggests that even among well-educated college students there was substantial dislike and disdain for some animals that are rare and endangered. Just because an animal was rare did not mean that everyone liked it, although it would be interesting to repeat the experiment today and see whether 20 years of conservation education had changed people's views. It would therefore be far more difficult to educate the public about visitor impact

Table 2.1 Popularity rankings for animals

Ranking	Animal	Proportion of like responses	Popularity rank
1	Horse	0.99	1
2	Dog	0.98	2
3	Deer	0.98	2
4	Human	0.98	2
5	Cardinal*	0.94	5
6	Seal	0.94	5
7	Pheasant	0.93	7
8	Cow	0.91	8
9	Goat	0.90	9
10	Salmon	0.88	10
11	Eagle	0.84	11
12	Fox	0.84	11
13	Gopher	0.80	13
14	Pelican	0.80	13
15	House cat	0.77	15
16	Mountain lion	0.74	16
17	Falcon	0.70	17
18	Bobcat	0.64	18
19	Wolf	0.61	19
20	Mouse	0.61	19
21	Crow	0.58	21
22	Pig	0.58	21
23	Hawk	0.58	21
24	Alligator	0.47	24
25	Vulture	0.31	25
26	Shark	0.30	26
27	Spider	0.29	27
28	Snake	0.28	28
29	Rat	0.22	29
30	Scorpion	0.20	30

*A striking North American wild bird
Source: After Bart (1972)

on snakes, let us say, than visitor impact on deer. People might simply care less. This also accounts for the fact that relatively few attractions featuring captive wildlife are based around rodents, amphibians and reptiles compared with those involving more user-friendly furry mammals.

Some species have no tolerance for people and are therefore not seen (mountain lion, wolf). Others have periodic need for seclusion and some are very tolerant. Large animals and birds are generally more popular than smaller ones and more colourful animals are more attractive than the drab (Shaw and Copper 1980). There is some evidence to suggest that 'frightening' species also attract visitors. Algonquin National Park (Canada) has a successful programme of wolf howls where wolves answer the call of park guides.Visitors, it seems, welcome the opportunity to hear the animals, even if they can seldom see them.

Wildlife-watching tours involving large mammals are common; those focused around frogs or spiders are rare since the creatures are smaller, less attractive and more difficult to see. However, with the expansion of the wildlife-watching market this is gradually changing as more and more minority interests are being served. But you would still have difficulty in enrolling for a full snake-watching holiday as insufficient people like snakes to make such a tour economically viable and anyway snakes are infrequently visible. People who like snakes often have to be content with visiting snake farms and serpentaria where snakes are bred for venom production, unless they are lucky enough to live near a facility like the Desert Museum near Tucson (Arizona, USA) with its excellent snake and reptile displays. Far more is known about the effects of visitor disturbance on mammals, for example, than on invertebrates or reptiles. Mammals are easier to see and easier to study and it is sometimes assumed (probably wrongly, according to some ecologists) that the impact of human visitation on mammalian communities is more severe than, say, on reptiles. However, there is still remarkably little definitive information separating impact due to visitors from other environmental influences, such as habitat destruction, listed above. The primary cause of disturbance on insects, amphibians, reptiles and small mammals is deliberate or accidental habitat destruction rather than gratuitous hassle from visitors. The fact that many of these creatures are seen by the public as dangerous or unpleasant, rather than being sought out as the objectives of a wildlife-watching trip, means that relatively little attention has been paid to their problems. This is exemplified by issues facing the saltwater crocodile population of southern Florida which was endangered not just by tourists but more significantly by hunters. Most visitors saw the crocodiles either as dangerous predators or as floating handbags. It was difficult to raise support for the creation of crocodile sanctuaries in the southern Everglades near Miami where the saltwater crocodiles breed. However, crocodile sanctuaries were eventually designated as protected areas, and made off-limits to visitors during the crocodile breeding season. Thanks to this policy saltwater crocodile populations are recovering nicely and also providing an educational visitor experience for the small number of officially guided tourist boats allowed past the sanctuaries at less sensitive times. Alligators, similarly disadvantaged in the public eye, have not been so fortunate. Baby alligators are still popular as pets, often discarded when they get too big to manage – hence the horror stories, apparently apocryphal, of giant alligators flourishing in New York sewers. But in Florida and the southern states where alligators are common in the wild discarded pets have become habituated to human company and feeding. The strangeness of alligators fascinates visitors who sometimes under-estimate the speed with which so large an animal can cover the ground, especially if the visitor has a dog, resulting in the regular poaching (by alligators) of tourist pets. There are also accounts of tourists straying off the beaten track and being eaten by alligators but these, too, are probably fictional. Both crocodiles and alligators are now farmed in the USA and several regions of Africa. This has halted unlimited hunting in the wild and provided alternative tourist attractions, although purists (including the writer) question whether raising such animals in captivity is ethical.

Wildlife disturbance by visitors

Visitor activity can adversely affect all types of wildlife, from lions to leopard sharks. Sporadic research on visitor impacts has been carried out since the 1980s (MacKinnon and MacKinnon 1986) and an example of the kind of categorisation produced can be seen in Table 2.2. From this we can see that the some significant visitor impacts on wildlife are accidental (such as noise pollution, careless use of fire causing habitat destruction) whereas others (such as feeding animals) are deliberate and may cause significant behavioural changes. This basic model has been modified by various writers to fit particular situations and Table 2.2 shows a version produced by Sindiyo and Pertet in 1984 as part of their study of disturbance in Kenya's protected areas. They categorised visitor disturbance as being either direct or indirect. Direct impacts result from vehicle speeding, off-road driving or night driving which may kill animals as well as initiate ecological changes. Cheetah and lion are reported to decrease hunting activity when surrounded by more than six vehicles. Even a foot safari will disturb animals and can also produce trail erosion. Sound, such as noise from radios, was a source of irritation and visitor litter a positive aesthetic and health hazard (Myers 1972). Indirect impacts included the collection of firewood which could result

Table 2.2 The potential effects of tourism in protected areas

Factor involved	Impact on natural quality	Comment	Example
DIRECT:			
1 Overcrowding	Environmental stress, behavioural changes	Irritation, reduction in quality, need for carrying capacity limits	Amboseli
2 Overdevelopment	Development of rural slums, excessive artificial structures	Unsightly, urban concentrations	Mwea, Keekorok, Ngai, Ndeithya
3 Recreational use			
(a) Power boats	Disturbance of wildlife and peace	Vulnerability during resting seasons	Kuinga Marine Biosphere Reserve
(b) Fishing	None	Competition with natural predators	Lake Turkana
(c) Foot safaris	Disturbance of wildlife	Overuse and trail erosion	Mt Kenya, Kickwa Tempo area in Mara
4 Pollution			
(a) Noise (radios, etc.)	Disturbance of natural sounds	Irritation	Many areas
(b) Litter	Impairment of natural scene	Aesthetic and health hazard	Many areas
5 Vandalism	Mutilation and facility destruction	Removal of natural features, fossils, facility damage	Sibiloi
6 Feeding of animals	Behavioural change	Removal of habituated animals	Mara, Samburu, Amboseli
7 Vehicles			
(a) Speeding	Wildlife mortality	Ecological changes	Amboseli; Nairobi, Masai
(b) Driving off-road	Soil and vegetation damage		Mara
(c) Night driving	Soil and vegetation damage		
INDIRECT:			
1 Collection of firewood	Small wildlife mortality and habitat removal	Interference with energy flow	All areas
2 Roads and Murram pits	Habitat loss, drainage changes	Aesthetic scars, disruption	All areas
3 Power lines	Destruction of vegetation	Aesthetic impacts	Tsavo
4 Artificial waterholes and salt provision	Unnatural wildlife concentration, vegetation damage	Replacement of soil required	Aberdares, Tsavo
5 Introduction of exotic plants	Competition with wild plants	Public confusion	Many areas, Mt Kenya, Elgon

Source: After Sindiyo and Pertet (1984)

in the death of small mammals, as well as the construction of artificial waterholes (see below, p. 66) distorting normal feeding behaviours. Since that time the impact of such apparently harmless activities as balloon safaris has also become apparent. Not only do balloon flights actively encourage off-road driving since they have no predetermined landing spots but various species of animals (particularly lion and buffalo) are terrified of the sudden noise from hot-air balloons with inevitable behavioural disruption (Cook 1988).

Few attempts have been made to quantify the levels of disturbance and the few relevant zoological field studies have been carried out on mammals. Experiments have been done, for example, using heart rate telemetry to determine the reaction of big game to disturbance by tourist vehicles. This enabled researchers to measure the levels of alarm or harassment felt by the animals from their increased heart rate. The resulting data was used to estimate animal energy requirements and the time the animal required to recover. Such work, although fascinating, is only of use in tourism planning if its results are used to generate a visitor management strategy whereby visitation levels or visitor behaviour are controlled at well below the predetermined stress levels (Cohen 1978).

All animals, not just large mammals, suffer from stress as a result of disturbance but this may be very difficult to measure. Bird communities are subject to disturbance by fishermen and incautious watersports users. Their activities can have a considerable impact on nesting birds such as ospreys, eagles and colonial nesting seabirds by frightening the birds from their nests in the breeding season. The solution is simply to restrict access during nesting. There are also suggestions that careless camp site and trail location may have an impact on songbirds but this seems to stem more from necessary habitat modification than deliberate harassment. Since birdwatching tours are becoming more and more popular it is to be hoped that further quantitative research will become available on this topic. The benefits of maintaining undisturbed bird and wildlife communities which are still open to visitors can be very considerable. Canadian researchers estimated that 10 000 people came to see the annual flocking spectacle of swallows at Pembroke, Ontario. Benefit–cost analysis (benefits exceeded costs by 4:1) suggested that the net tourist value of the site was C$ 520 000. Around 17 000 birdwatchers visit the Point Pelee National Park to see the spring bird migration, providing revenue estimated at $6.3 million in 1987 (Hvengaard et al. 1989).

Keen birdwatchers are now able to take a variety of purpose-built tours from seabird watching in the Orkneys to photographing birds of paradise in Irian Jaya. 'Birders' are generally recognised as amongst the most responsible of wildlife watchers as they are generally the best informed and most interested in conservation. Birding is an intrinsically less intrusive activity than motorised safari tourism, for example, since it can only be satisfactorily carried out in quiet conditions by relatively small numbers of unintrusive people. Birding was very important in the initial development of Costa Rica's wildlife management strategy and large numbers of birders were among the first ecotourists attracted to the country. The continuous strength of birding groups and a guaranteed market were responsible for the construction of many Costa Rican lodges and the development of ground operator businesses. Birding influenced nearly every aspect of the environmental movement of the country in a positive way because most of the groups were science based. National Park managers felt that their impact was positive, not merely creating habitat disturbance, since they knew how to behave in a park and were also willing to share their experience such as answering questions about species migration. Their political power was useful, too, and many returned to organise funding for park projects (Baldares and Laarmen 1990, Laarman and Perdue 1989).

Wildlife habituation

Not all wilderness visitors are so well informed or so careful to avoid adverse impacts. The desire to maximise the possibility and closeness of an encounter has led in some cases to the deliberate habituation of certain species, sometimes with encounters deliberately 'staged' for human benefit. A wild animal becomes habituated when it is gradually conditioned to accept the presence of human intruders and modify its behaviour accordingly. This may be beneficial, enabling human visitors and wildlife to co-exist with minimal disturbance, but it may also be destructive if animal behaviour is modified by the provision of food lures. In theory a successful habituation programme enables humans and wildlife to co-exist with the animals accepting humans as a harmless element of their environment. In Costa Rica's Carara Biological Reserve, for example, scarlet macaws and white-faced capuchin monkeys are very tolerant of visitors and stay close to trails giving tourists an excellent view. This seems to have been achieved with no adverse impacts on their habitat or behaviour. However, excessive visitor pressure can also habituate animals in a way that is quite undesirable. Most people are familiar with photographs from African National Parks showing cheetah families draped over tourist vehicles. The cheetahs have lost their fear of humans and accept the vehicles as part of their normal environment although the eventual cost to their species may be high (below, p. 66). In many protected areas habituation is simply a case of wildlife becoming accustomed to seeing visitors. Sometimes this is artificially induced, occasionally for the benefit of the animals but more usually for the benefit of the visitors. Perhaps the most famous examples of habituated animals are the mountain gorillas of east Central Africa where wildlife biologists spend years habituating the 'show' gorilla families before they see a tourist. Such habituated gorillas then ignore the presence of visitors whose revenues are contributing to the upkeep of both habituated and 'wild' gorillas elsewhere in the parks of Rwanda, Zaïre and Uganda. This is discussed further in a detailed case study (below, p. 62). In the case of the gorillas deliberate habituation has clearly contributed to the survival of their species, as well as providing a high quality visitor experience. The case study below examines an equally famous example of habituation from the Rocky Mountains of North America (Herrero 1970, Cole 1974, Gilbert 1976, Jonkel and Servheen 1977). Here bears have been accidentally habituated by roadside feeding, with consequent behavioural alterations. The consequent traffic 'bearjams' for which Yellowstone National Park (USA) is famous are the result of bears becoming habituated to humans by this process.

Bear habituation in North America

The bear populations of the magnificent Rocky Mountain National Parks of the USA and Canada have produced an excellent example of animal habituation. Managing human–bear interactions in wilderness areas involves managing people as well as bears. Habituated black bears in the Rockies stop traffic, beg food and destroy camp sites. Grizzly bears attack hikers and wilderness campers and polar bears threaten tourists. When human–bear contacts are constant and not harmful to the bear the animals become accustomed to people and lose their fear. This neutral conditioning is easily followed by aggressive or exploitative behaviour by bears to humans, especially if the former can obtain

Bear habituation in North America (*continued*)

food. Exploitative aggression is taught to young bears by adult females and this cultural deterioration can spread through a whole population. Reversing the trend is difficult. In certain circumstances, as with the polar bears of Churchill, Canada, it may be possible to separate bears from visitors but it is usually necessary to develop management plans which involve the co-operation of both parties. After nearly 30 years of debate some recommendations have emerged on which bear biologists agree. These are turned into comprehensive information leaflets and displays and issued to visitors in the form of advice, not regulations. A typical leaflet might tell tourists that in order to avoid unwelcome attention from bears they should:

- eliminate garbage
- cook and hang food away from camping areas
- avoid surprising bears by making a lot of noise in areas of low visibility
- be careful when walking into the wind and where there is noise from wind or running water
- never linger in areas obviously used by bears
- never put grizzlies in a position where they feel threatened.

New people in bear country need to obey these simple rules and exercise common sense as well as being briefed about what to do if attacked by a bear. Grizzly bears present the worst problems. Grizzlies and people can only co-exist where contact between them is intermittent, the people do not carry much food or try to approach the bears. Tens of thousands of perfectly safe nights are spent by hikers and campers in unprotected areas where the human populations are low and the bears are occasionally hunted. This has led to recommendations that permit occasional grizzly hunting under proper management which keeps the bears wary of people and eliminates those with aggressive tendencies. In preserved areas the situation is very different owing to increased backcountry use and development pressure which increases human–grizzly contacts and changes the behaviour of both species. People put a high value on just seeing a wild grizzly or knowing

Bear habituation in North America (*continued*)

that they are there. The developing role of wilderness management is to reduce the likelihood of, and prepare visitors for, an unexpected confrontation. Methods include restricting or controlling the numbers of people in key areas of grizzly range and planning trails which avoid popular bear crossroads, feeding grounds or breeding areas. There is no failsafe answer for avoiding problems with bears, only intelligent management and encouraging visitors to make greater efforts to learn more about them.

In some cases bears can be successfully separated from humans to their mutual advantage. Canada's largest population of polar bears makes an annual migration along the Hudson Bay coast of northern Manitoba with the result that the town of Churchill has become known as the 'polar bear capital of the world'. The surrounding area is arctic tundra, treeless boreal forest of the Canadian Shield and visitors may also see caribou, arctic fox, wolf, arctic hare, lemmings, snowy owl and gyrfalcon. During the polar bear season, starting mid October, Churchill receives an enormous percentage of the visitors on which its economy has now become dependent. At the same time the town is occupied by highly dangerous semi-habituated polar bears who have become a nuisance. Each year some invade houses causing persistent offenders to be tranquillised and removed by helicopter. Tourists are highly vulnerable to these aggressive carnivores and the ground handlers of Churchill have solved the problem by utilising specially designed 'tundra buggies' to separate bear and human. These vehicles, standing 2 m tall on huge rubber tyres, have a minimum impact on the tundra vegetation and can seat up to 36 people. They become surrounded by curious predatory bears providing wonderful photo-opportunities with minimum risks. The success of these bear management methods has meant that all accommodation in Churchill is booked months in advance and some tourists are accommodated in 'bear camps' up to 45 km away. One of these consists of linked units joined like railways cars in order to be bearproof and equipped with shooting platforms for photography.

This case study clearly shows that managing habituated animals requires a variety of different approaches, depending on the animals concerned, animal and visitor density, type of visitor activity and local environment. It also shows that managing wildlife generally goes in partnership with managing people to provide solutions to the problem of adverse interaction. Animals can learn to accept predictable types of disturbance if these are harmless and do not inflict stress. Habituation, as we have already seen, is a management method possible with certain species in National Parks and refuges. It can be exceptionally successful, as in the case of the mountain gorilla. Even outside protected areas such as alongside roads animals may become habituated to the sight and sounds of vehicles, not showing any concern unless the vehicle stops. Not all animals can become habituated. Some species become intolerant of humans at specific places (like favourite feeding grounds) or at specific times of year (especially the mating or breeding seasons). Others dislike being directly approached or forced to make eye contact. Some animals (especially primates) dislike being photographed. These things can easily be explained in an information sheet or briefing for visitors to a protected area but, perhaps surprisingly, few tour companies include such information in their details but leave it up to individual guides. Making prolonged eye contact with a gorilla, for example, is seen by the gorilla as a direct threat and visitors are counselled to keep their eyes lowered and their movements subdued. A wise visitor mimics the body posture of the gorilla and makes no sudden movements that could alarm the animal. Habituation can also be reversed. Game birds are increasingly difficult to shoot as the hunting season progresses since they have learnt good survival responses. It has even been suggested that animal behaviour could be modified genetically to increase or decrease habituation as required. At one point it was considered whether to experiment genetically with some caribou populations in Canada that were not being attacked by predators. The idea was to produce a docile population suitable for public viewing by selecting for animals that were exceptionally difficult to hunt and 'harvesting' (killing) wary, nervous animals. Fortunately this was never carried out.

It is also possible partly to habituate animals and alter their distribution in relation to humans by altering the habitat. Animals living near human activity can be attracted by the provision of food. This is, after all, the basis for garden birdwatching, probably the most popular wildlife-based hobby. Attractive grassland areas near forest or mountain cabins can be made more attractive to animals by the use of natural fertilisers to attract more deer and other grazers. This policy has been followed in many US parks to draw elk and deer to public viewing areas. It can also be used for the opposite purpose: distracting animals from areas where there are problems with human interactions.

The provision of food lures to attract animals is frowned upon by biologists but it is widely practised even in protected areas. At the Samburu Lodge in the Samburu National Park (northern Kenya) it is possible to sit on a shady verandah and watch a goat being slaughtered and hung up to attract crocodiles and leopards at night. The provision of this bait provides wonderful photo-opportunities although more sensitive visitors do find the idea of a dead animal being used as bait quite repellent. This concept was taken further in one of the Indian National Parks which received a very bad press for using live goats as bait for tigers. This idea was transmitted into fiction with the tethered goat used as a bait for Tyrannosaurus Rex in the film *Jurassic Park*. Unfortunately, using bait and food lures is still a common occurrence in real life, justified as maximising visitor pleasure and the chances of getting a good photograph especially when the animals involved (such as crocodiles) are normally relatively torpid. One of the more bizarre occurrences comes from the desolate hilly island of Komodo in Indonesia where there is an unusual wildlife attraction – dragons. These 'dragons' (actually large monitor lizards, *Varanus komodoensis*) can grow up to 3 m long and weigh 130 kg. They were made famous by David Attenborough in his film *Zoo Quest for a Dragon* made in 1956 and have since received a steadily increasing stream of visitors. More than 1000 'dragons' are to be found on Komodo and the nearby islands of Rinca, Padar and north west Flores. The dragons hunt live prey as well as feeding on rotting carcasses and in recent years their diet has included at least one careless tourist who ignored advice not to leave the tourist camp without a guide. The camp is run by the PHPA (the Indonesian government department responsible for managing nature reserves and national parks) who also provide a dead goat to attract dragons. Although the experience is not for the squeamish in ecotourism terms its adverse impacts are minimal. The dragons ignore their visitors, the visitors get a decent photograph and everyone from local farmers to tour guides gains some monetary reward. The only party to suffer is the goat.

Another form of 'bait' is the recording device which is a popular means of attracting birds or mammals with distinctive calls used by less scrupulous tour operators. Costa Rica has a problem with such operators who use sound lures to extract large amounts of money from clients by presenting an unnatural variety of birds. The practice has now been outlawed and inserted into the environmental regulations governing nature-based tourism.

Establishing carrying capacity

In order to quantify the type and degree of disturbance that an animal community is receiving from visitors we need to establish its 'carrying capacity', a term unfortunately defined differently by different interest groups (Getz 1983). The carrying capacity of an area or ecosystem might be its:

- biological (or ecological) carrying capacity
- tourist or visitor carrying capacity
- accommodation and transport carrying capacity
- psychological carrying capacity.

Biologists arrive at a figure which respects the ecological limitations of a site by placing a limit on the number of visitor days permitted in order to preserve the integrity of a natural resource base. Ecological carrying capacity is reached when changes in wildlife behaviour are observed or when species begin to disappear or other changes like soil erosion become obvious (Clark and Gilad 1989). Ecological carrying capacity can be influenced by human-induced observable disturbance such as changed animal behaviour (e.g. outmigration, altered nesting patterns). An overall reduction in the number of species present is also a clear sign. The governments of host countries often have a more flexible approach and less scientific way of establishing carrying capacities. Their maximum figures may reflect the need to maximise short term foreign exchange earnings even if this destroys the resource base in the long term. Accommodation carrying capacity is fixed by bedspace availability and transport carrying capacity by the number of passengers that can be transported. Psychological carrying capacity is the level beyond which visitor satisfaction drops as a result of overcrowding. This has been exceeded by a large margin in many East African National Parks causing dissatisfaction and loss of business to less crowded parks in southern and south west Africa. Host social carrying capacity is the level beyond which unacceptable change will be caused to local cultural stability and attitudes towards tourists.

Perhaps the best general definition for our purposes is that carrying capacity is 'the maximum level of visitor use an area can accommodate with high levels of satisfaction for visitors and few negative impacts on resources' (McNeely and Thorsell 1987). To calculate this figure it is necessary to establish maximum use estimates (which is difficult). In practice many planners rely on defining what constitutes a 'tolerable level' of visitation which can be sustained over time. Estimating the carrying capacity of a park or protected area simply in terms of visitor days is insufficient. The maximum sustainable capacity of an area requires the careful planning of geographically separated access points and placement of tourist facilities to avoid excessive contacts between different groups visiting the park at the same time. Issues of seasonality need to be incorporated, within both animal and human communities.

Much attention to the problems of estimating carrying capacity has been given by the WTO (WTO/UNEP 1992) who recommend a formula (Boullon 1985) for estimating tourist carrying capacity as

$$\text{Carrying capacity} = \frac{\text{area used by tourists}}{\text{average individual standard}}$$

(the denominator is usually expressed as persons/metre^2) which is carefully defined for each case by evaluating psychological and ecological capacity. From this one can derive a total of daily visits as

$$\text{Total of daily visits} = \text{carrying capacity} \times \text{rotation coefficient}$$

where

$$\text{Rotation coefficient} = \frac{\text{no. of daily hours open for tourism}}{\text{average time of visit}}$$

In order to determine environmental factors it is necessary to know the following:

- size of area and usable space
- fragility of environment
- wildlife resources
- topography and vegetation cover
- behavioural sensitivity of certain species to human visits.

Not all the area may be usable space as some might be inaccessible. The fragility of soils is very variable with loose sands (as seen in coastal dunes) being exceptionally vulnerable. Wildlife resources will not be uniform over the area and will vary in distribution and diversity according to the season of the year. Topographic factors such as different forms of vegetation will affect capacity; thick bush can conceal large numbers of both animals and people (increasing environmental capacity) whereas visitor concentrations on flat, open savanna are very obvious. Additionally, some species are especially sensitive to the presence of visitors, a factor which is additionally affected by their degree of habituation (p. 25).

It is possible to make a similar list of variables which determine social carrying capacities, which include:

• viewing pattern
• tourists' viewing choices
• visitors' opinions
• available facilities.

Visitors are never evenly distributed across an area. A study in Amboseli (Henry 1979, 1982) suggested that 90 per cent of visitors used only 10 per cent of the area, and that 50 per cent of use occurred between 15.30 and 16.30 in the afternoon. Tourists' viewing choices are partly determined by the available species but also by the tourists' own interests. Big cats, animals nursing young, mating, dying, feeding or hunting are magnets for visitors. Views about how present crowding levels are rated can be established by a simple survey, and quantifiable variables such as available bedspaces from simply counting. Such information can help management to increase carrying capacity. It may be possible to design new viewpoints, tracks or trails to spread visitors over a wider area or to reduce conflicts between competing use by zoning. Visitors' opinions can be utilised to improve the provision of information and interpretation facilities and access can be aided by the use of more durable materials for heavily used resources such as trackways.

The use of carrying capacity for management planning and the avoidance of animal disturbance involves establishing the management objectives regarding the social and environmental conditions which are to be provided (Inskeep 1991, WTO/UNEP 1992). Some aspects of the carrying capacity of an area can be modified. The physical carrying capacity of an area, for example, can be increased by hardening, fencing or walkway construction. Its psychological carrying capacity (how crowded it seems to visitors) depends on many factors including the prior expectations of visitors and the nature of the terrain. In order to generate a successful management plan it is really necessary to know what the situation in a park or wilderness area visited by nature tourists was like before the tourists arrived. This can then be compared with existing and projected situations to establish the appropriate visitation level. Unfortunately, there are very few studies of carrying capacities made before parks or other protected areas are established and most calculations are made after a problem has become apparent. This lack of initial data has led to a proliferation of methods to regularise affairs when it becomes clear that carrying capacities have later been exceeded (Clark 1991). Solutions may be drastic. If significant disturbance is detected areas or entire parks may require restricted access. Pasachoa National Park in Ecuador closes for one month each year for recuperation and to give the park's ecosystems a rest from visitors. Many other areas have an effective recovery period in their low season or coinciding with especially sensitive times such as nesting or breeding seasons, although these may be the most attractive to visitors. Few protected areas are equally popular for visits all year round and tourists may be largely absent during the monsoon or rainy season when access is tricky. This allows areas and communities to recover from disturbance.

Because it is so hard to measure carrying capacity disputes frequently emerge between different sets of vested interests such as tour operators and park managers. Most protected areas do not have the facilities to utilise even the simplest measurement techniques such as establishing the frequency of site visits, the size of groups, their length of stay, activity patterns and any observable effects on animal behaviour. A surprisingly large number of protected areas have no visitor statistics at all let alone reliable quantified observations on animal disturbance or the effects of visitors. Carrying capacity figures can also be ignored. In the original management plan for the Galapagos carrying capacity was estimated at 12 000 but when demand increased so did the designated capacity (to 36 000) simply by ignoring the original figures. Carrying capacity calculations also involve looking at visitor concentrations and dwell times at different locations within protected areas. The carrying capacity of Amboseli National Park was estimated as the park's vehicle capacity, since that is the mode of transport for visitors. The final figure of 95 000 vehicles a year was derived from a calculation involving park size, the desired level of vehicle density and assumptions about visitor behaviour and preferences. The effect on animal communities was, obviously, of paramount importance. However, just because an area is operating at less than its calculated maximum capacity does not mean that it will not feel crowded as all the vehicles present could be compressed into a relatively small area of the park (Henry 1979, 1982). Nor does the fact that maximum capacity has not been achieved mean that the existing visitation level is causing no problems for animals.

Carrying capacity can be increased by management procedures such as encouraging wet- or off-season use (generally by differential pricing, see p. 128) and making fragile resources such as trails and viewing centres last longer by increasing durability. The use of carrying capacity calculations can help in developing a sustainable management plan for protected areas and suggest ways in which this figure can be achieved and managed with minimal impact on wildlife. But like all management solutions, the policies are only as good as their level of enforcement.

Questions

1 What methods are available to establish the level of visitor disturbance experienced by wildlife?
2 Design a research strategy to be used in an investigation of the significance of roadside feeding of bears in the Rocky Mountains.
3 In what ways can wildlife harass tourists, producing a reduction in the quality of the visitor experience?
4 Discuss the ways in which carrying capacity calculations can help in devising a management strategy for a protected area.

3
Managing visitors

Visitors need to behave in a fashion acceptable to wildlife, not the other way round. This is true irrespective of the context of the encounter, whether it is a protected area, local park, aquarium or zoo. However, it is much easier to influence visitor behaviour inside a National Park or reserve than it is outside in areas which may have multiple access. In order to achieve a high quality of visitor experience while minimising the impact of that experience on wildlife it is necessary to consider what the nature of that impact might be. Broadly speaking we can consider four types of adverse impact:

- visitors disturbing or harassing wildlife
- visitors disrupting feeding or breeding behaviour
- visitors polluting the natural environment
- visitors killing wildlife (usually by accident).

In order to combat these potential problems visitors need to be managed in accordance with four basic principles, namely:

Separation (physically separate visitors from wildlife)
Integration (mix visitors and wildlife by careful management of their interaction)
Participation (allow visitors to participate in wildlife management schemes
Education (provide more information about the consequences of adverse impact).

Clearly, most successful visitor management schemes may involve a combination of two or more of these principles. The idea of educating the public, for example, works on the theory that the more people know about the behaviour of a species or ecosystem the more likely they are to support measures to conserve it. This is thought to be true even if such measures limit individual freedoms, although in practice the amount of inconvenience that visitors appear to be prepared to put up with seems quite limited. Little objective research has been done on the subject. Management schemes or education programmes may be ineffective if some powerful factor intervenes which attracts visitors to the environment even if their visit has detrimental effects. If a species is designated as endangered people will overturn their normal behaviour patterns and value systems in order to see it. If an area has been recently opened some visitors will pay large sums to go there, even if the potential consequences of their visit are severe. An example of this is discussed further on in this chapter where the effect of tourism on Antarctica is considered.

Many of the adverse impacts of visitors on wildlife are quite accidental. Few tourists wish to cause any harm to the species or environment which they visit but may be quite ignorant of the effect of their actions. This is seen below in a consideration of the effects of diving tourism on coral reefs and leisure boating on marine mammals. Many people are unaware of the potential impact on wildlife of such harmless pursuits as rambling or riding. Even domesticated animals and dogs accompanying tourists can have an impact on wildlife. Pack and saddle animals such as the horses used in pony trekking inhibit wild ungulates' use of meadows, consume feed and introduce exotic species of vegetation. This can be controlled by limiting the use of certain areas, choosing appropriate camp sites and if necessary providing supplementary feeding for wildlife (Ream 1978). Compared with the effect of motorised transport the impacts are relatively minimal. Dogs accompanying walkers in wilderness areas can frighten ground-nesting birds and kill small animals – as in the UK where dogs accompanying ramblers regularly cause problems for upland farmers in the lambing season. But dogs also have positive benefits for outdoor visitors, providing companionship and increasing human perception of the natural environment through their reaction to sounds and smells. Dogs may also be used as work animals and there is currently a rash of tour operators offering 'wilderness mushing' holidays in North America using sled dogs. In fact the very last sled dogs to leave Antarctica were

WHALE
WATCHING
GUIDELINES

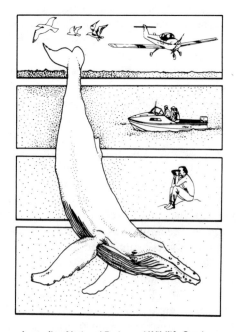

Australian National Parks and Wildlife Service

Figure 3.1 Whale-watching guidelines

destined for Hudson Bay to provide rides for tourists. Successful visitor management schemes may involve a combination of separating visitors from visited, either by zoning (in the wild) or construction of barriers such as park boundaries, enclosures or cages. Visitors may be

How to approach a whale

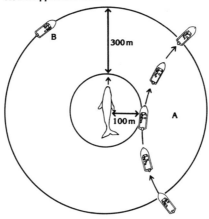

Caution

* When whale watching, accidents may occur, especially if the whales feel threatened or harassed. Active whales also require ample space particularly during the mating season when males competing for females may engage in rough physical contact.

Limits of approach

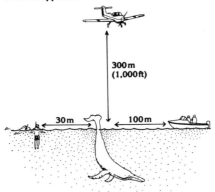

encouraged to participate by helping in conservation programmes, controlled animal feeding or research projects. Integrating animals with their visitors may be achieved harmoniously by environmentally sensitive transport, such as the substitution of horse, elephant, foot or camel for the intrusive motor car. Each context, environment and species creates a different set of visitor management problems and opportunities.

Marine environments present a special series of problems due partly to their great size, the difficulty of policing any regulations and the wide variety of activities that they include (Salm and Clark 1984). Compared with terrestrial habitats we know virtually nothing about human impact (let alone tourism impact) on marine environments. Even swimmers can unwittingly pollute a marine environment. For example, the lagoon at Xel-Ha south of Cancun on Mexico's Caribbean coast is a natural aquarium cut out of limestone which forms a breeding centre for thousands of species of tropical fish. It includes lagoons connected to one another by underwater currents and clusters of enormous parrotfish surrounding the entrance to an underwater Mayan shrine. Not surprisingly this is a prime tourist attraction, extremely crowded at the peak of the tourist season with buses taking day-trip visitors from nearby Cancun. Xel-Ha is crammed with divers, snorkellers and glass-bottomed boats causing a noticeable diminution in water quality. In order to protect these breeding grounds from pollution due to boats and suntan oil and stop disturbing the lagoon's population of nurse sharks and stingrays part of the area has been designated an underwater preserve. Even here diminished water quality is evident since the ban on fishing makes the lagoon especially attractive to large numbers of snorkellers. Exactly the same problem is faced in Hawaii's famous Hanauma Bay, only an hour from downtown Honolulu on the island of Oahau. This shallow lagoon is renowned for having some of the friendliest fish in the Pacific including the splendidly named humuhomunukunukukuapuaa ('fish with pig-like snout') which will eat out of your hand. However, the continued popularity of Hawaii as a tourist destination means that the fish of Hanauma Bay are also being threatened by disturbance and suntan oil. Despite management strategies including the imposition of a daily visitor quota (cars can be seen queuing by the roadside often from early morning) it is difficult to control numbers and there are many complaints about local people being excluded.

Educating visitors

Effective education about the effects of wildlife harassment requires an assessment of the level of knowledge about wildlife possessed by each

Figure 3.2 Diver with stingrays, Cayman Islands

visitor. Disturbance and harassment can often be reduced if the visitor understands the impact of his or her activity and is offered an alternative. Basic information can be issued to visitors at the access points to protected areas or made available at visitor centres. Education does not necessarily mean that people will make the right choices. Despite publicity that noisy airboat rides in wetland habitats such as the Big Cypress Natural Preserve in Florida disturb wildlife and cause distress to nesting birds, many visitors, however, still see taking a ride across the swamp as an ecologically friendly activity. This includes a certain element of laziness when it comes to transportation. Most methods of environmentally friendly transport require energy (such as substituting a canoe for the airboat). It follows that a successful visitor management scheme is likely to combine educating the visitor with regulating visitor activities, but such schemes have to be policed in order for them to be effective (Tabata 1989). Here is an example of a visitor code developed by Costa Rica, which tells tourists what the effect of their activities might be and points out potential impacts (such as smoking in protected areas) that many might have been unaware of. When it comes to educating visitors about wildlife Costa Rica, with a total of 72 protected areas covering more than 1 million hectares (21 per cent of the country), probably has the best set of guidelines for responsible wildlife tourism in the world. The visitor is being encouraged to become an active participant in conservation by patronising guides and tour operators who obey these guidelines and to consider the effect of his or her choices on the environment and species that he or she is visiting. The code is not only designed to protect the environment but also to provide security for the visitor and maximise the quality of his or her experience (Quesada-Mateo and Solis-Rivera 1990, Tangley 1986).

A visitor code for Costa Rica

- Book with a qualified tour or ground operator.
- Ask the guide's qualifications.
- Don't book into fragile areas during prime courtship and mating seasons or in the first weeks of rearing young. If you don't know when this is ask the tour operator.
- Refuse to enter a protected environment with more than 15 people in your group. Recommend splitting the group or discuss alternatives.
- Stay on marked trails no matter what others say.
- Report anyone taking biological specimens.
- Don't smoke in canopied forest or near wildlife.
- Whisper or communicate with hands when near wildlife, don't talk loudly.
- Don't use flash in an enclosed forest environment especially if the subject is rare or endangered.
- Don't throw or drop anything beside trails, even biodegradable materials.
- Don't play radios or electronic devices that make foreign sounds in protected areas.
- Don't enter a private or public protected zone without the permission of the guard on duty or in the company of a licensed qualified guide.
- Keep off anything that might resemble a field research project in a park or reserve. This might include a net, box, screen enclosure, cloth cover, etc.
- Don't purchase orchids, artifacts or biological specimens.
- Don't drink water from an open source.

Separating visitors from wildlife

Areas can then (theoretically) be managed to separate visitors from wildlife if both the people and the wildlife allow this. It is possible to alter utilisation patterns by signs and regulations during the course of the year in order to cope with critical periods (such as breeding seasons).

Complementary methods include controlling visitor numbers and access. It is much easier to manage a small remote area for the mutual benefit of wildlife and visitors than it is to control a large multi-access area often containing various different ecological zones. Saiwa Swamp National Park was set up in northern Kenya to preserve just one animal, an aquatic antelope called the sitatunga. Here the remote location makes it easy to eliminate day-trippers. This is helped by the fact that sitatunga are very shy and seen only at early dawn or dusk. Moreover, there is no accommodation or tourist facilities in the park (with the exception of a water tap and long-drop toilet) and numbers are restricted to a maximum of 20 overnight campers. Visitors must camp in a central area and are then free to explore the small park on marked trails which terminate in hides overlooking swampy areas. Minimal disturbance is guaranteed by the fact that the sitatunga are extremely nervous and frightened by the slightest noise. So if visitors fail to be unobtrusive they will also fail to see the animal which is their objective. It is ironic that this little park has become a popular stop for overland tour buses as well as naturalists. The reasons for this are that entrance is cheap and the location ideal for a tour bus travelling around the protected areas of northern Kenya into Uganda. Overland passengers are less fussy about the quality of their accommodation and quite willing to camp, but the lack of hotels or infrastructure means that the more up-market safari visitors are absent. The park has achieved its objective – to safeguard the home of a single rare species with minimal disturbance – but it also produces minimal revenue.

The waters off the Caribbean coast of Florida contain mainland America's only coral reef. Florida's coral reefs are among the world's most biologically productive ecosystems. Here the area has been protected as part of the marine sanctuary programme with a management plan which designates recreational spots for diving and sportfishing and also supports commercial industries including fishing and kelp harvesting. The Florida Keys National Marine Sanctuary was created in 1990 to protect 2800 square nautical miles (7250 km^2) on both sides of the Keys, a chain of coral islands linked by a road joining Key West to Key Largo. This is now the second largest marine sanctuary in the USA. The Looe Key Sanctuary, 5.32 square miles (13.6 km²) in area off Big Pine Key, was designated in 1981 and is famous for its clear water and moderate sea conditions which produce exceptional visibility. The area is therefore suitable even for novices and attracts 60 000 divers, snorkellers and fishermen each year. There are special regulations prohibiting divers from removing or damaging natural features, marine life or archaeological resources. They must not anchor (except in designated areas), discharge bilges, use wire fish traps, explosives, spear guns or dangerous weapons. Detailed guidelines inform visitors about the effects of accidentally standing on or touching coral. Visitors are asked not to hand-feed the fish (who are friendly) because of the chances of causing an accidental injury and altering behaviour. Hook and line fishing is permitted within designated limits but there is no collecting of coral, shells or starfish. The regulations are effectively policed by fast patrol boats who can enforce fines for damaging coral or running aground. Boats must show a dive flag and restrict their wake within 100 yards (91 m) of such a flag, for safety reasons. In the core areas of the sanctuary further restrictions are in place and only diving, snorkelling, swimming, photography and boating are allowed with fishing banned.

Despite the fact that we are now increasingly aware of the problems that are caused by poor visitor management schemes new areas are constantly being opened to visitors without proper study or guidelines. In many cases the areas involved are so vast (like the Amazon Basin) that it is difficult to conceive of visitors causing more serious environmental damage than the activities of, say, mining or logging operations. Such assumptions lead to a degree of complacency which has resulted in a lack of hard data concerning visitor environmental impact damage. Very often such damage was not predicted and only considered after it had occurred. As we have seen tour operators, particularly those in specialist fields such as ecotourism or adventure tourism, require a constant stream of innovative destinations to tickle the palates of jaded environmental tourists. Today's discerning nature tourist who may already have spent a decade of vacations touring the world's great National Parks needs to be offered increasingly remote areas. Visiting these areas will not be cheap but at the top end of the market the consumer is willing to pay a high price for near exclusivity. As we have already seen wildlife tourism destinations continually go on and off line in conjunction with political and environmental changes, as well as the dictates of fashion. This means that an innovative tour operator in the mid 1990s must already be looking for destinations that can be researched to develop new products as much as a decade away. Access to remote areas will be increased by more use of air transport such as helicopters and seaplanes with the result that few areas of the world will be truly inaccessible.

The following short case study summarises the impact of tourism on one of the world's last great wilderness areas, the Antarctic, where a radical overhaul of existing tourism management practices is clearly very necessary in the face of projected visitor numbers (Hall 1992, HRSCERA 1989, Snepenger and Moore 1989, Thompson 1977, Wace 1990).

Wildlife tourism in Antarctica

Antarctica represents one of the last tourism frontiers: a frozen continent and contiguous southern ocean which covers 10 per cent of the world's surface area. Its extreme climate and physical conditions deterred continuous human occupation until the middle of the 20th century but those same harsh conditions and corresponding natural beauty are now attracting visitors in ever increasing numbers. Antarctica, though not under the legal control of any country, is regulated by the International Antarctic Treaty signed in 1961 to control the management of its resources. In the 30 years which have elapsed since the signing of the treaty Antarctic tourism has become a significant issue and control measures relating to tourism are now being considered.

The first tourist flight to Antarctica took place in 1956 and visitation levels have increased steadily since then to the current level of around 2500–3000 per year. Cruises are the most popular form of tourism, generally originating in Chilean or Argentinian ports such as Punta Arenas. This fledgling tourism industry is predicted to experience significant growth, aided by television programmes such as the recent BBC series *Life in the Freezer*. Concern is being expressed about uncontrolled tourism disrupting national scientific programmes, both through the mere presence of

Wildlife tourism in Antarctica (*continued*)

visitors and the need to offer emergency services with concomitant legal problems concerning insurance, jurisdiction and liability.

Antarctica's wildlife is certainly under threat from tourism; how great that threat becomes depends on the tourism management strategy adopted. Antarctica remains the last near-pristine continental wilderness with unique marine and terrestrial ecosystems where at least 60 per cent of terrestrial and 70 per cent of marine species are endemic to the continent. Observed impacts on wildlife are summarised in Table 3.1.

Regular low overflights of penguin colonies have been known to cause panic, stampedes or desertions of nests with considerable loss of eggs by crushing or from subsequent predation by skuas (HRSCERA 1989, p. 10). Ship-based tourism is hard to regulate and cruise travel in the Antarctic summer coincides with the peak breeding season for many species and may disturb the wildlife breeding sites that are a key feature of attractiveness to visitors. Ships can pollute over a wide area through waste and sewage disposal and oil spills. In January 1968, for example, the tourist ship *Magga Dan* ran aground at McMurdo for several days and the *Linblad Explorer* has twice run aground in the Antarctic peninsula. Wildlife sites are affected by constant visitation with the likelihood of behavioural change and denudation of habitat. Adélie penguin numbers were halved in Cape Royds between 1956 and 1962 owing to the constant landings of tourist helicopters which brought them up to five loads of visitors per day. A similar stampede resulted in the deaths of 6000 king penguins on Macquarie Island in June 1990 caused by humans disturbing the birds.

Increased control of tourism probably means more land-based facilities. This development of a tourism infrastructure will inevitably take place near Antarctic bases and disturb research. An international convention is needed to regulate tourism in the Antarctic replacing the existing recommendations for codes of behaviour which cannot be enforced.

Table 3.1 Environmental impacts of tourism in Antarctica

Type of activity	Nature of impact	Infrastructure characteristics
Overflights	Exhaust fumes and oil pollution from engines; engine noise disturbs wildlife	No requirements for permanent land-based facilities
Ship-based	Transient environmental effects: oil spills; disturbance to wildlife; potential introduction of bird and plant diseases and exotic flora	No requirements. Pressure on regularly visited land-based facilities
Onshore	Increased demand for ice-free land and fresh water, sewage and rubbish disposal. Site degradation with high visitation. Possible combination with scientific bases? Also has ship-based impacts	Needs all-weather airstrips for large commercial planes

Source: After Hall (1992)

Integrating visitors and wildlife

It is easier to take a minibus on safari than to use a horse or go on foot, even if the latter are permitted. And, as we have already seen (above, p. 37), even travelling on foot disturbs animals. However, in cases where the managers of a protected area have resisted allowing motorised transport the quality of visitor experience has markedly improved. But in some large areas this simply is not possible. There is the additional point that vehicular transport enables the visitor to cover a lot of ground and therefore maximise his or her chances of seeing a broad range of species. A traveller on foot runs the risk of not seeing anything. There are a number of successful compromises including the solution adopted in the Royal Chitwan National Park in Nepal where elephants are utilised as park transport. Not only is the elephant silent and undeniably environmentally friendly but riding on elephant back enables the visitor to watch tigers in safety, if he or she is lucky.

A great deal of publicity has (rightly) been given to the problems being experienced by areas such as the Great Barrier Reef in Australia. There diving tourism, combined with a series of other natural hazards such as the effect of land pollutants, has had a disastrous effect on the reef (Salm and Clark 1984). Corals are delicate structures composed of millions of individual animals called polyps. They grow slowly, as little as one inch (2.5 cm) a year for some species. A living coral reef is the most diverse marine ecosystem in the world but it is also fragile and vulnerable. Divers destroy coral by touching it or breaking off pieces for souvenirs. Coral colonies can be damaged by careless anchors or pollution from bilges. The fish inhabiting the reef can be threatened by spearfishing or collecting for aquaria, despite the fact that tropical fish collected from the wild generally die within a year. Fortunately, on the Barrier Reef careful and continuous monitoring combined with zoning and education programmes have had a very beneficial effect. A similar response was taken in the USA where the National Marine Sanctuaries Programme was established in 1972 to promote comprehensive management plans for marine areas of special ecological, historical, recreational or aesthetic significance. Initially eight areas were selected including open ocean and inshore coral reefs. These varied in size from 1 to 1252 square nautical miles (3.4 to 4294 km^2). Monterey Bay in California was recently added to the total. This bay, located 50 miles (80 km) south of San Francisco, is effectively a submarine canyon whose rich environment supports whales, fish, otters and seabirds including both warm-water and cold-water species. The newly designated sanctuary is closely integrated with the work of the $50 million Monterey Aquarium (p. 111), one of California's major tourist attractions. Here visitors can enjoy feeding the sea lions lolling off Fisherman's Wharf and watch sea otters (only recently reintroduced into the area) at play in the harbour. The museum and sanctuary support a large sightseeing boat industry which functions all the year round and takes tourists to watch whales between December and January. The aquarium itself has 100 galleries and exhibits include a reconstruction of sanctuary underwater kelp forest. It is the centre for a very extensive scuba diving industry of considerable economic significance and the spearhead of an underwater management programme that permits multiple use so long as this is balanced with measures to maintain the health and integrity of the ocean.

   In some cases it is necessary to develop visitor management plans to control both voluntary and involuntary interactions between visitors and wildlife. A case in point is the Florida manatee (or sea cow) which is an endangered species whose problems stem from the fact that it not only chooses voluntarily to interact with humans but inhabits an environment which is becoming pressured by increasing volumes of tourism. This case study (below) looks at methods which are being used to solve the problem, combining education with separation (by zoning). Unfortunately, this may come too late for the last remaining manatees (Shackley 1992).

The Florida manatee

The endangered manatee (sea cow) population of southern Florida is under stress from many directions, particularly from a spectacular rise in water-based tourism activities. These huge, slow-moving gentle mammals spend their lives grazing sea grass beds in the shallow coastal waters. Adult manatees may reach 13 feet (4 m) in length and weigh over 3000 lbs (1360 kg). During the winter manatees move inland through river estuaries and often congregate in natural warm springs or the discharge areas of power generating plants. Manatees share their coastal habitat with increasingly large numbers of water-borne tourists. Florida has an annual increase of 5 per cent in boat registrations and by the year 2000 there will be more than 1.75 million registered boat users in Floridian waters plus up to 5 million people participating in water-based recreation. Florida now leads the USA in recreational fatalities, 2.5 times the national average with more than 12 000 boating accidents taking place each year. The amount of water remains constant but more, faster boats mean more collisions, excessive speed and marine traffic congestion. Boats also kill manatees, who are so frequently injured that animals which survive contact with boat propellers bear scar patterns sufficiently distinctive to be used for identifying individuals. Manatee mortality and injury rates from boat propellers are rising at 25 per cent per year and 10 per cent of the total surviving manatee population was killed in a single year (1989). Manatees are sometimes chased by boats and harassed by divers as well as entangled in discarded fishing lines. The Endangered Species Act of 1973 set up 27 protected areas for manatees including 'no entry' coastal zones and designated warm-water refuges. Careless boating, violating diving codes or ignoring idle speed zones or sanctuary limits result in a fine. The National Parks offer interpretive programmes to increase awareness and there is extensive media coverage of the manatee's problems. The rehabilitation programmes for injured

The Florida manatee (*continued*)

manatees at Homosassa Springs Park (western Florida) and Miami Seaquarium are popular with visitors although unfortunately their patients cannot be released into the wild as they are unable to follow the annual migration routes into warmer water and quickly die.

Part of the manatees' problem is that they are so friendly, choosing voluntarily to interact with people, visiting marinas to receive gifts of lettuce and a hose-down with fresh water. This brings them into dangerous contact with boats. The region around Crystal River and Homosassa Springs where manatees are especially common has become the centre of a thriving manatee-based diving industry. At the height of the manatee season (November–March) these waters may have a diver density of 1 diver/10 m^2 of water. Here the animal's friendliness is once again exploited by irresponsible divers who will stroke, try to ride and tease the animals. Visitor guidelines have been produced recommending people to snorkel, rather than scuba dive, since manatees are disturbed by the bubbles. This advice is often ignored by dive shop owners since snorkelling is a less profitable activity. Manatees are an important factor in the economy of the catchment area where 25 hotels and 300 food service establishments cater for tourists engaged in water-based recreation.

Enforcement of regulations, the establishment of a manatee phone hotline to report dead or injured specimens, voluntary education programmes and commercial sponsorship of manatee rehabilitation schemes are all being tried in an effort to save the remaining animals. Their survival ultimately rests on the effective policing of the safe area policy with funding increases to the Florida Department of Natural Resources to enforce an extended protection strategy. Projected ways to raise revenue are a tax on new propeller-driven boats. Without these measures the Florida manatee could easily become extinct by the end of the century. It is ironic that the final nail in the manatees' coffin is being produced by the large numbers of diving tourists and snorkellers who come to visit them.

Visitor participation

Another set of management solutions to problems presented by wildlife disturbance actively involve visitors with the species that they have come to see. On a simple level this can involve selected feeding of species in zoos, aquaria or in the wild (p. 30). Another way to do this is by conservation holidays, specially designed to enable visitors to become actively involved, or so-called adoption programmes for wild animals (particularly dolphins, orang-utans, elephants and gorillas) to foster bonding between humans and endangered species. The method is used by conservation organisations to raise funds for specific programmes by involving the person intimately with the fate of his or her chosen animal. Many such organisations also run study tours to increase involvement at different scales from local birdwatching with the Field Studies Council to a complete range of professional tours with the American Audubon Society or Sierra Club. As members of Earthwatch volunteers can spend their holidays tracking wolves in Carpathia, conserving sea turtles off Bahia in Brazil, studying the life of the Caribbean mongoose or monitoring the whale populations of Madagascar. Earthwatch is the world's largest organisation which matches paying volunteers with scientists and archaeologists who need help on research and conservation projects. Each year it fields 400 teams from 50 countries with volunteers often paying several thousand dollars for the privilege.

Some areas have become very well known for active conservation tourism projects. The turtle islands north of Sandakan (Malaysian Borneo) include some of the most important turtle breeding places in south east Asia. In 1977 a marine park was created around three of the best islands to include their surrounding waters and reefs. Green turtles come ashore at night to dig a hole with their flippers and lay around 100 eggs, watched by anxious visitors. Rangers then transfer the eggs to a temperature-controlled hatchery for the 50–60 day incubation period and at the appropriate time another batch of visitors are able to watch the hatching and assist the babies to reach the sea. Even so only 3 per cent will survive disease and predation to reach maturity but the females will return in 20 years to the same beach. Since the conservation programme is now 30 years old green turtle numbers are flourishing and providing a nightly spectacle for their visitors. It is, however, doubtful whether visitor efforts significantly affect the hatchlings' chance of survival but the visitor is rewarded with the feeling of having achieved some positive conservation benefit. Turtles and turtle eggs are emotive issues – whole communities can become involved in their conservation. Some years ago it was realised that sea turtles emerging at night become disorientated because of artificial light sources along the shoreline, increasing mortality. The problem became severe with high density coastal hotel developments near turtle beaches. Although some communities from Queensland to Florida have experimented with restricting beachfront lighting at hatching time it was impossible to eliminate it completely on densely developed beaches without compromising the safety of people using the beach. Research found that it was possible to devise artificial lights which could be seen by people but not turtles and some of these have now been installed (Witherington and Bjorndal 1991). Costa Rica also makes good business from sea turtles which nest in several parks and bioreserves. Several different species may be seen: giant leatherbacks, hawksbill, green and olive ridley turtles at different times of year on the Pacific and Caribbean coasts. Access to the exact locations is restricted during the turtle nesting periods (*arrivadas*). This protects the turtles from outside pressure at that crucial time when they arrive to nest on the same beaches where they were hatched 20 years before. Qualified guides take small groups to the nesting sites, briefing them about the disturbing effects of light, noise, movement and sounds.

Undeniably, active participation in a research or conservation programme contributes to the welfare of the species while providing a very high level of satisfaction for the visitor. This issue, the nature of visitor experience, will be discussed in the following chapter.

Questions

1 Design a visitor code for tourism to the Antarctic and suggest how this could be policed and implemented.
2 How do you think visitors to the UK's National Parks could be made more aware of the potential effect of their activities?
3 Why is it more difficult to manage visitors in marine than terrestrial environments?
4 Make a survey of the conservation holidays currently being advertised in your country (get your information from tour operators and advertisements). Do these holidays have any real benefits for the wildlife being visited?

4
The visitor experience

The degree of satisfaction felt by a tourist is partly derived from pre-existing circumstances and conditions combined with the influence of his or her personality. For example, a visitor arrives at a destination equipped with a series of expectations and motivations shaped by his or her perceptions of the area and a whole complex of social, cultural and economic circumstances. The quality and nature of the satisfaction that the visitor experiences is determined by the match between reality and expectations. However, this match can be influenced by a number of other factors such as:

- time constraints
- tiredness and speed of recovery
- speed of adaptation to a new environment
- personality and social skills
- illness
- commitment to success.

A tourist who is tired or jet lagged from a long journey or constantly being rushed from place to place in the course of a demanding schedule is less likely to record his or her experience as satisfactory than a visitor who had a short, uneventful journey with a planned period of adjustment to his or her new environment. Most travellers have limited amounts of time available and wish to maximise the quality of their holiday experience within this period, whether this is a two-week wilderness tour or a day trip to a safari park. The tourist's initial expectations and constraints of time create an eagerness to learn and explore a new locality but also result in intolerance of inferior service which wastes time (Ryan 1992). Since many wildlife-watching holidays are not only tiring but also crammed with activities that leave little time for adjusting to new environments this puts great pressure on the provider of the holiday to supply a high level of service quality. Minor illnesses associated with food, sun, drink or insects often mar the nature of the visitor experience, as does association with other tourists with different and potentially conflicting motivations. An example of this is discussed below in the context of guest ranches in Africa which experience conflicts in accommodating both visitors who want to watch or photograph wildlife and guests who are primarily motivated by the opportunity for big-game hunting. The most successful ranches have specialised in one group or the other, just as the successful wildlife tours are usually composed of visitors sharing common motivations and expectations (such as a group of birdwatchers).

Visitor satisfaction results from a match between expectation and perception but how individual visitors deal with this gap is influenced by their commitment to the success of the holiday (Graefe and Vaske 1987). In a nature-watching holiday the level of commitment is typically very high but the visitor also has very high expectation levels from the service provider. If such expectations are not met then the experience will be rated as unsatisfactory. If, for example, a tourist has decided to take a day trip to watch whales then that tourist will be most disappointed if no whales are seen. On the other hand this discontent can be ameliorated if the service provider takes immediate action such as diverting the boat to watch other marine wildlife or offering refunds or a second trip free. Some wildlife-watching holidays demand a level of skill from their participants. These may be physical skills (required for trekking, climbing, diving) or mental skills such as the level of knowledge necessary to get the best out of a specialised activity (such as a highly focused botanical tour). In such cases if the level of challenge exceeds the skill of the participant (i.e. the trip is too hard) then dissatisfaction results. Similarly, if the level of skill or expertise required exceeds the challenge provided then the tourist gets bored and dissatisfied. Tourists are now very experienced at being tourists, which puts a great deal of pressure on tour operators to provide high levels of service quality (generating satisfaction) without creating any additional environmental or sociocultural pressures on either host environment or

Figure 4.1 Whale watching

communities. The nature of the visitor experience creates a satisfactory feeling about the holiday (or not) which feeds back into the system and shapes the nature of demand for the next trip. It therefore follows that the more experienced the tourist the more likely he or she is to be very demanding.

In most cases the tourist travelling abroad is culturally a permanent outsider and instantly recognisable as such. The sense of being a tourist is obviously felt most strongly in mass tourist centres such as crowded resorts and least so in remote wilderness areas. The tourist needs to find satisfaction by establishing an identity for him- or herself in this situation and in a mass tourism context this is often accomplished by relating to other members of the group rather than the host community. In determining the level of tourist satisfaction we find that the quality of experience derived from relationships with other people is often more important than that derived from contact with host communities. In the case of nature tourists seeking a wilderness experience the quality of that experience may also be influenced by the absence, rather than the presence, of other people and a poor level of satisfaction is therefore recorded where areas are too crowded or crowded with people doing some activity which the tourist in question finds disagreeable. This accounts for problems which may be generalised as concerning 'conflicts of use'. A further factor in the overall nature of the experience is the relationship between tourist and service provider. For the visitor this is unique and interesting whereas for the provider the individual visitor is merely part of an anonymous mass. As we have seen the level of satisfaction of that visitor increases with an increase in individuality. Hence the fact that the success of a visit (whether a holiday of merely a day trip) is often heavily influenced by the nature of the relationship established with tour guide or tour organiser (Almagor 1990).

These observations about the nature of tourist satisfaction underpin the case studies utilised in this chapter. In the case of visitors going to see Rwanda's mountain gorillas, for example, the outstanding levels of satisfaction usually recorded partly derive from the fact that expectations have been exceeded by reality. Additional satisfaction is gained from having overcome physically demanding conditions and also from the relative exclusivity of the experience which contributes prestige. The visitor is part of a small highly motivated group which has generally been travelling together for some time and adjusted to its different component personality sets. Visits to gorillas have usually been carefully prepared by background reading and the only problems resulting generally derive from a perceived lack of information provided. The second case study looks at the nature of visitor experience in Etosha National Park in Namibia. Here, high satisfaction levels derive from the fact that tourists have often previously visited the National Parks of Kenya and Tanzania which are viewed as crowded and overcommercialised. Etosha gives the visitor a feeling of being alone in an African savanna while still having the benefits of adequate accommodation and a decent infrastructure. Visitor expectations are therefore generally exceeded. The final section of this chapter looks at the nature of destructive visitor experience using examples from hunting, poaching and sportfishing. This raises the issue of how conflicting visitor expectations within the same environment can be managed. Since destructive tourism is an emotive issue it is also necessary to ask whether although such experiences generate high levels of satisfaction from the participants is this ethically permissible?

The wildlife tourist

Why do people want to walk on the wild side? Recent research suggests that nature-based tourism, even something so simple as walking in a country park, can give people what the psychologist Maslow called 'peak experiences', those existential moments that induce a heightened sense of being alive and make the visitor happier, more confident and less stressed. Being able to look at unspoilt wilderness areas seems to have considerable psychological benefits for the individual but it is an addictive pastime. The committed wildlife tourist must continually seek new areas to reinforce the pleasant experience and continually generate additional satisfaction. As we have already seen the experienced tourist is likely to demand high levels of service quality in order to gain high levels of satisfaction. Such experiences tend not only to be expensive but also to require time and preparation on the tourist's behalf.

Surveys of visitors to wilderness areas (e.g. Buckley and Pannell 1990) show that, hardly surprisingly, such people neither expect nor want any obvious 'development'. This agrees with what we have already surmised: that a high quality of wilderness experience can only really be enjoyed either in the absence of other people or certainly where other tourists are similarly motivated and engaged in related pursuits. The major problems which detract from wilderness tourism quality are

- noise (human or mechanical)
- visual impacts (ugly lodges or signage)
- crowding
- environmental damage

but at the same time visitors demand features which apparently conflict with this list, such as

- easy and relatively cheap access
- adequate visitor facilities
- high levels of safety.

Problems for wilderness managers therefore include the provision of adequate infrastructure which must also be non-polluting, unobtrusive and easy to reach. Different groups of visitors will achieve high satisfaction levels from different expectation bases. A first-time safari visitor, for example, will have different satisfaction levels from an experienced wildlife watcher. Most complaints from wildlife watchers relate to conflicts between different groups of visitors, especially between those who favour mechanised transport and those who do not. People have radically different perspectives about the ecological soundness of their own particular interests. As visitor densities increase at a particular site and the characteristics of an area change in consequence so do the type of people visiting the area and their expectations, levels of enjoyment and requirements. Eventually the wilderness experience is replaced by sport or outdoor socialising. Those who visited the area earlier in its life cycle are often dissatisfied with the changes and will not come again. This makes it difficult to monitor changes in the quality of visitor experience in any given area.

In 1988 the Worldwide Fund for Nature completed airport visitor surveys in five countries in South and Central America to see if it was possible to find out more about these 'nature tourists' visiting protected areas and National Parks (Boo 1990). The results suggested that nature tourists come in two main varieties:

- those primarily motivated by an interest in conservation
- people adding a wilderness day trip to a business or family visit.

Both categories of tourists were asked about the motivation for their trip and three levels of motivation were discerned. Highly motivated people said that the existence of the protected area was the main reason for their travel decision whereas the less motivated said it was very important but not vital. People with low levels of motivation said that the presence of a protected area was only slightly or not important to them. Some of the results of the survey are summarised in Table 4.1 contrasting the motivations of wildlife and leisure tourists. From this we can see that the nature tourists were:

- slightly older (aged 43.9 vs 40.8) than leisure tourists
- more evenly split along gender lines than conventional visitors
- often making their first visit to a country
- more likely to travel in small groups rather than as individuals
- also, if highly motivated, more likely to enjoy visiting cultural sites.

The fact that such visitors were slightly older than comparable groups probably reflected the fact that such holidays are expensive and older people may have more leisure time and available cash. Many were travelling in small special-interest groups, as might be expected, and the fact that they tended to be visiting a country for the first time reinforces the point, made above, that wildlife tourists continually search for new

Table 4.1 Background information collected in WWF airport surveys, 1988, according to high, medium, and low priority categories

	High	Medium	Low
Average age	43.9 (72)	41.8 (76)	40.8 (187)
Gender:			
Male	51% (45)	55% (52)	63% (219)
Female	49% (91)	45% (42)	81% (37)
First visit to country	73% (91)	63% (95)	51% (220)
Travel with:			
Alone	21%	31%	32%
Family	36%	36%	33%
Friends (colleagues)	23%	18%	27%
Tour	20%	15%	8%
(N)	(91)	(95)	(221)

destinations. The study also concluded that the most popular nature-watching activity was birdwatching. Even among the poorly motivated nature watchers as many as 50 per cent admitted to enjoying birdwatching and others in the same group still participated in nature-based activities such a taking jungle or boat trips. High levels of satisfaction were recorded with the most frequently requested improvements being better information provision and transportation. However, if the visitor is really motivated he or she will not be deterred by inadequate access roads like those in the Monteverde Cloud Forest Reserve (Costa Rica) although the quality of the experience might be impaired. For some visitors poor access, remoteness and inadequate infrastructure was a positive bonus. The survey reinforced the point that such visitors seek information; they are not motivated simply by curiosity nor by a desire to be entertained. Few National Parks in the developing world are able fully to satisfy this thirst for information which is expensive to provide. It is certain, though, that nature tourism has tremendous educational potential which is not being fulfilled.

Mixing with the animals

Figure 4.2 summarises the nature and variety of wildlife-watching experiences. Essentially these can be divided into two: where the

	Captive	Free	
Observation	Zoo Aquarium	Safari Game drives Diving Whale watching	Nature of tourist activity
Participation	Feed zoo animal Interactive zoo exhibits	Gorilla watching Swim with dolphins Hunting	

Nature of animal captivity

Figure 4.2 The nature and variety of wildlife-watching experiences

animals are free or where they are held in captivity. However, there is a continuum of function between these two extremes. What constitutes freedom? We would all agree that an animal confined in a zoo cage was not free but neither are animals wandering in a safari park, although their enclosures have larger territories. Wild dolphins are free, as are the fish encountered by divers, but are the animals in a National Park free? Few National Parks are entirely fenced and many have permeable boundaries permitting the animals to move in and out. But this is not always the case – the animals being observed by guests at Treetops Lodge are advertised as wild but unlike the tourists their exit from the park is made impossible by a 450 volt electric fence and a 3 m ditch. Although visitors to a large game reserve see animals apparently living natural lives they are actually contained in a giant enclosure – albeit one positioned at the ecologically acceptable end of a continuum which starts with zoo cages. We can use the same model (Figure 4.2) to classify a visitor to a wildlife-based attraction who may be either an active participant or merely a passive observer. Again, there are many intermediate stages. Clearly, far more people are going to be able to be passive observers of captive animals in zoos than active participants in dolphin swims. Active participation need not necessarily be a good thing – destructive activities such as hunting would also come under the heading of active participation. However, the highest quality of experience often comes with active participation, where the visitor feels that he or she is achieving some kind of temporary affinity with a different species or its environment. With captive animals this kinship is fostered by such devices as permitting visitors to feed certain animals under controlled conditions or 'adopt' a particular animal for whom they become responsible. In the wild such matters are much more difficult to arrange since unscripted interactions are difficult to manage and have considerable cost and safety implications. It is, for example, far easier to control the activities of a group of tourists watching wildlife from a safari minibus than it is to cope with a similar group travelling by foot. Yet the second activity is infinitely more rewarding since the visitor obtains the opportunity of entering the animal's habitat, rather than observing it from the safety of his or her own. As we have already seen the highest satisfaction levels can be obtained from visitor experiences which permit the visitor to become an unobtrusive part of a wilderness environment. This is extremely difficult to achieve, bearing in mind the limitations of access, safety and infrastructure already discussed. Sometimes such interactions may happen by accident, such as a backpacker encountering some interesting species in the course of a wilderness hike, but more often such meetings are orchestrated and planned. The accidental encounter, after all, generates no profit for a tour company whereas a planned encounter may be very profitable indeed. Higher levels of visitor satisfaction are reported, for example, by divers or swimmers interacting with dolphins in their wild habitat than by visitors to aquaria where the dolphins are captive. Captive dolphin shows are becoming less popular than they were, largely because of the many ethical reservations expressed about keeping marine mammals in captivity. The supposedly healing properties and psychological benefits derived from swimming with dolphins have generated many locations where visitors can swim with captive animals. These range from the tacky to the very well managed as in those cases where the dolphins are free to return to the wild at will. Swimming with wild dolphins is becoming increasingly popular and can be semi-formalised by tour operators taking visitors to areas where such encounters are the most likely. In the rare cases where dolphins take up semi-permanent residence near a coastal town they can underpin an entire tourism industry. One famous dolphin was recently the victim in a bizarre case where a tourist was charged with sexual molestation. The bottlenose dolphins of Monkey Mia in Shark Bay, Western Australia, have been fed from the beach by tourists since the late 1960s. Their tolerance of humans was exploited by scientists led by Dr Richard Connor from the University of Michigan who developed a research programme to study them in the wild (Dowling 1991). Ten years and a hundred dolphins later the programme has contributed tremendous insights into our understanding of dolphin family life as well as supporting an entire tourist industry. The opportunity to interact with a completely wild animal in this way is extremely rare but even in cases where such interaction is slightly staged it may provide the very highest quality of experience. The following case study examines the issue of mountain gorilla watching in Rwanda which not only generates high levels of visitor satisfaction but also provides revenue for the conservation of the species being watched (Fossey 1983, Cavalieri and Singer 1993, Harcourt 1979–80, Lee *et al.* 1988, Shackley 1995).

Tourists and the mountain gorilla – the ultimate visitor experience?

Until the recent tragic events in Rwanda visiting one of the world's last remaining populations of mountain gorillas in the Parc National des Volcans was the wildlife watcher's ultimate experience, generating almost universally high levels of satisfaction. It was not cheap; an organised trip from the UK would cost at least £1500 and an independent traveller paid a minimum of $150 per visit just for a permit. Since the amount of time spent with the gorillas was limited to one hour per party this constitutes a very expensive day trip. The mountain gorillas live in dense bamboo forest up to altitudes of more than 4500 m in the Virunga mountain chain. They were extensively studied by Dian Fossey whose life was romanticised in the film *Gorillas in the Mist* which provided an immense boost to gorilla tourism. Without her efforts and subsequent cash provided by visitors gorillas would be extinct in Rwanda (and the current political situation makes it impossible to take a census). Even before the civil war gorillas were at risk from poaching and habitat pressure (local people wanting more agricultural and grazing land). Despite the expense and considerable exertions required (often an eight-hour climb up through 3000 m of thick rainforest) gorilla visits were frequently booked out months ahead. The great success of the experience seems partly due to the rarity of the species, partly to satisfaction at having completed an arduous trip, but mostly to the startling effect of suddenly seeing gorillas in the wild. The thickness of the forest means that the visitor literally pops up in the middle of a gorilla group, able (though forbidden) to reach out and touch an

Tourists and the mountain gorilla (*continued*)

enormous male silverback gorilla. Few visitors reported being frightened and many found the experience deeply emotional. This seems to be attributable partly to the near humanity of the gorillas (visitors often recounted feeling a sense of kinship) and partly to the complete lack of any visitor facilities, a sense of being completely alone in the wild with a magnificent and totally wild creature. In order to maximise this effect four groups of gorillas had slowly been habituated to visitors over a period of many years, with the result that they completely ignored human beings, which gave visitors the sense of being invisible. The visitor felt part of the gorilla's environment, and members of gorilla groups thought nothing of pushing a human visitor out of the way to reach a tempting bamboo shoot. Visitor group sizes were small (maximum of eight visitors) and the guides and guards helpful and well informed. Visitors felt amply rewarded for both effort and expense and many could not wait to repeat the experience. Visiting gorillas is not generally something done by first-time nature tourists but often by those who had previously experienced the bustle of the big National Parks and contrasted the gorilla experience very favourably. Yet the high quality was achieved without any luxury (there was no convenient comfortable accommodation) and required considerable personal exertion. What is the real secret of its success?

Watching the animals

Not everyone wishes to make the physical effort necessary to become a temporary part of a gorilla family, and for many tourists a high quality of experience can be gained by just watching, and photographing, without either the need or desire to interact. This may often be accomplished from within the (relative) comfort and safety of a motor vehicle, as in the safari industry of East and southern Africa. Animal-loving visitors to these and other National Parks or protected areas, wherever they are, have certain requirements:

- plenty of different animals to see
- safety and peace of mind

Figure 4.3 Photographing moose

- good reliable transport
- good photographic opportunities
- not too many other people
- plenty of information and a good guide.

Unfortunately the requirements of park managers may be rather different. They have to cater for all the visitor requirements just listed as well as to produce revenue, some of which will be used for conservation purposes. This has to be done with no adverse tourism impacts on the park environment or its animals. The tourism experience has to be managed within a framework of seasonal variations (both in tourists and climate) and increasing visitor numbers. Visitor transport has to be managed giving paramount importance to the needs of the animals, not the tourists. This is easier said than done.

Let us consider the issue of transport, since so much observation of animals (rather than participation) involves motorised transport of one sort or another. One of the great problems prejudicing the quality of visitor experience in some of Africa's National Parks (particularly the longer-established and more accessible parks in Kenya) is lack of control over visitor transport. Park roads can be churned up by a medley of family saloons, Land Rovers and ubiquitous zebra-striped microbuses. These microbuses are operated by privately owned tour operators, not park staff, who do not necessarily give the highest priority to conservation and will break rules to get near some interesting animal in the hope of receiving a sizeable tip. Such transport satisfies many of the quality visitor criteria such as comfort and safety but in practice their quantity detracts from the visitor experience owing to overcrowding and obviously adverse effects on animals. Such large numbers of vehicles destroy the grass on which grazing animals and the whole food chain depend. It is easy to generate regulations to prevent such problems but a different matter to enforce them since the parks are huge and inadequately staffed. In the 1980s Amboseli National Park was granted aid from the World Bank only if tourists were successfully confined to marked roads, but this is difficult to police. Other methods, such as the construction of roadside ditches and stoneblocked tracks have also been tried to confine visitors to designated areas but they are generally unsuccessful (Western 1982, 1986).

Are visitors sensitive to the welfare of the animals providing their

Figure 4.4 Tourist minibuses converging at a single location in Samburu National Park, Kenya

high quality experience? Empirical evidence would suggest that this is not necessarily so. The writer once watched 23 minibuses converge at a single location in Samburu National Park, Kenya (Figure 4.4), after the reported sighting of a cheetah and cubs. The clouds of dust generated by speeding drivers frightened off much of the game and thickly coated roadside plants. The drivers ignored track boundaries and parked anywhere (engines running) so that their passengers could get a good view. The cheetah, who had been in the process of making a kill, was frightened off and unable to feed its cubs, one of whom was limping and probably injured. A few more missed meals and its survival would be in doubt. The mother was therefore forced to expend useless energy without being rewarded by a meal. Did the visitors feel satisfaction that they had seen a cheetah or guilt that their presence had deprived the cheetah family of a meal? There is evidence from many parks that cheetahs are actually changing their hunting patterns. They normally hunt at dawn and dusk which is unfortunately the same time as game drives so they have adapted to hunting during the heat of the day. Unfortunately this requires extra energy and creates additional stress for the animal. Not only cheetahs are vulnerable to this kind of pressure although large predators are among the worst affected. An extensive study of the tourism carrying capacity of Amboseli was carried out by Wesley Henry in 1980. Amboseli was already experiencing congestion problems and Henry found that 80 per cent of tourists were confining their activities to a 15 km^2 area at the edge of the park's woodlands and swamps. He considered that this might reflect the distribution of game but eventually concluded that 80 per cent of tourists' stationary viewing time was preoccupied by just six animal species with 50 per cent spent on lion and cheetah alone. Just as in the Samburu example (above), vehicles concentrate where the cats are.

The ultimate, non-participative animal-watching experience has to be that provided at the famous 50-room Treetops Lodge in Kenya's Aberdare National Park, which we have already mentioned. This has a roof terrace bar overlooking two waterholes floodlit at night with guests free to watch the animals feed while seating themselves in considerable comfort. The hotel even advertises game viewing 'the lazy way' whereby guests can opt to be woken during the night by a professional hunter every time one of the Big Five (lion, leopard, rhino, elephant and buffalo) is seen outside the hotel. This is not an experience that would appeal to all. Nor is it entirely ecologically sound as the animals around Treetops are not being viewed in the correct ecological balance with too many grazers and not enough predators. The habitat of the animals has been modified to create comfortable visitor accommodation. The waterhole is regularly topped-up during the day between one set of visitors leaving and next arriving. Each week two buckets of salt are deposited just below the lodge windows to lure animals to the lodge. Unfortunately the salt leaches out into the surrounding soils, killing plants and trees around the waterhole. Artificially high concentrations of animals are found around the lodge but there is little ground cover for shy species. At least the animals are safe from one thing – Treetops bans children under 7 'to avoid alarming game'.

In theory if a park or protected area is sufficiently large then its animal population is effectively living in entirely wild conditions. However, even Africa's largest reserves, which are enormous (the Masai Mara and Serengeti together cover more than 10 000 square kilometres), are not sufficient to cover all natural ranges and merely provide animals with artificial islands of protection. This smallness matters more to predators than prey – a wildebeest can survive on half a hectare of grass but a lion needs to eat 50 wildebeest per year. The ecologist Paul Colinvaux noted that in a 'natural' situation big fierce animals (primary tourist targets) are rare and their confinement to small islands can create problems requiring continuous habitat modification. In practice the visitor watching lions drinking at a Treetops waterhole is still in a large and magnificent zoo.

There have been many complaints in Kenyan parks by visitors who said that they came to see animals, not other visitors. Business is being diverted to South Africa, Botswana and Namibia where there are less tourists and a higher quality of experience (defined as the nearest that it is possible to come to a perceived natural state) may be obtained. The growth of the safari industry is still very healthy although in broad terms Africa still has only a small share of world tourism international arrivals but this is growing steadily. However, new destinations are continually opening. Unlike the African parks which generally require visitors to stay in a closed vehicle for their own safety Latin American parks can often be observed by walking through them, producing a much closer feeling of unity with the natural environment. Many of the Indian parks such as Namdapha in Arunachal Pradesh (Figure 4.5) utilise elephants as environmentally friendly transport. There is certainly a general world-wide trend in protected areas to get visitors away from their motors and onto their feet (or suitable alternatives) wherever possible, with immeasurable benefits for visitor and visited.

Figure 4.5 Indian elephants as environmentally friendly transport

The definition of a successful visitor experience must be related to the realisation or exceeding of expectations but as we have seen what is satisfying for the visitor need not be so for the animal or its habitat. The problem for managers of protected areas is to maximise the quality of the visitor experience while giving priority to the welfare of the park's inhabitants. The following case study looks at how this can be done (Shackley 1993).

Etosha National Park, Namibia

Etosha National Park is Namibia's major tourist attraction, covering more than 20 000 square miles (51 800 km^2) and sheltering 114 species of mammals and 340 species of birds. Unlike the East African parks Etosha never appears crowded although it receives around 45 000 visitors per year. Total annual revenue exceeds £2 million per year (from accommodation, gate receipts, catering and other services). All visitors are confined to motor

Etosha National Park, Namibia (continued)

vehicles. Tourism peaks in the dry season between April and October when game concentrates near waterholes. During the rainy season temperatures can easily reach 45°C, making a day spent in a stationary car less than attractive. The park is administered by the Ministry of Wildlife, Game and Tourism who control all facilities, including the supply of accommodation. Less than half the total area is open to tourists, with the entire area west of the Ozonjuitji waterhole (Figure 4.6) preserved as a conservation area. Tourists are restricted to the area immediately surrounding the massive 5000 km^2 saline flats of the Etosha pan, dry most of the year but occasionally home to flocks of flamingos after good rains. There is a network of narrow gravel roads surrounding the pan which wind through the flat savanna grassland and mopani woodland. The animals encountered include large populations of giraffe, lion and elephant, together with rarities such as black-faced impala, black rhinoceros and Hartmann's mountain zebra.

All visitors are required to register and obtain a permit at one of Etosha's two gates and to check in with the visitor centre at one of

Figure 4.6 Giraffes at the Ozonjuiti waterhole in Etosha National Park, Namibia

Etosha National Park, Namibia (*continued*)

the three rest camps, each 70 km apart. Park rules are strict: a 60 km/hour speed limit is enforced to protect both animals and plants. Between the hours of sunset and sunrise all visitors must be inside one of the three camps whose gates are firmly shut. People caught outside after this time can be expelled from the park as can anyone found outside their car. Roads are constantly patrolled by nature conservators so that there is very little off-road driving.

Although the concentrations of game are not so high as in Masai Mara or Serengeti there are relatively few visitors and, out of season, it is possible to spend a day there and see hardly anyone. The area is very large but well maintained and wildlife watching is facilitated by careful habitat management. Some waterholes are natural springs but many are artificial, constructed to attract game and provide a good view for visitors who can park within a few metres of the Big Five. Strategic placing of these waterholes effectively disseminates visitors round the park so that only those locations nearest to the rest camps are heavily used. Each rest camp has its own waterhole located just outside the fence – the one at Okaukuejo is floodlit for enthusiasts to continue watching all night. Each rest camp has a 'sightings' book indicating the best places to see favourite species and nature conservators monitor waterhole levels. Visitors drive from waterhole to waterhole stopping as they wish. By far the majority are individual family groups with few minibuses or larger vehicles. No guided tours are organised by the park management and the visitor is left to his or her own devices. The three rest camps offer camping or self-catering in blocks or rondavels (African-style thatched huts), in pleasant surroundings complete with restaurant and swimming pool. The largest camp, Okaukuejo, contains a major scientific research station and a small museum/exhibition for visits. All have information centres. Namutoni, in the east of the park, is a whitewashed Beau Geste-style fortress dating from German colonial days, offering visitor accommodation in rooms below the battlements, grouped around a shady courtyard (Figure 4.7).

Increased interest in Namibia has resulted in pressure on the tourist facilities of Etosha. Various strategies are planned. A

Etosha National Park, Namibia (*continued*)

Figure 4.7 Visitor accommodation at Namutoni in Etosha National Park, Namibia

fourth rest camp is being established at Otjovasondu, in the extreme west of the park, and the Ministry plans to open new tracks into previously wildlife-only zones in order to reduce pressure on the existing network. Such a move would enable visitors to drive across the whole width of the park, more than 300 km. New waterholes are being constructed to control the movements and concentrations of game animals. Park accommodation is also beginning to suffer from competition with privately owned luxury hotels on ranchlands just outside the two gates. This is producing a new use pattern where visitors on inclusive tours stay at these hotels and enter the park on day trips. Part of the reason for this is lack of investment in upgrading park accommodation to international standards. Accommodation in Etosha remains basic, the park is not crowded and habitat modification, although present, is unobtrusive. The park is one of Africa's most successful visitor experiences.

The primate problem – good experience, bad ethics?

Chimpanzees, gorillas and orang-utans as our closest living relatives are inevitably fascinating to the wildlife watcher. This fascination has increased with DNA revelations concerning just how close that relationship is. Humans and gorillas, for example, share more than 98 per cent of their DNA. Today, there is a well-defined movement which argues that the great apes, because of this genetic kinship, deserve to receive the basic ideas of equality extended to humans. Any reader interested in the ethical and moral issues surrounding this point is recommended to read the essays collected in *The Great Ape Project* edited by Cavalieri and Singer (1993). The closeness of our genetic relationship with great apes doubtless accounts for the fascination they exert but also raises problems related to ethical issues surrounding the keeping of apes in captivity and the conditions under which apes should be observed in the wild. As we have seen the habituated gorilla groups of Rwanda contribute considerable tourism revenues into the Parc which are used for the conservation of their species. Until 1993 the system remained a shining example of wildlife earning its own living at minimum environmental cost. Today it is impossible, for political reasons, to visit Rwanda's mountain gorillas but on the Zaïre and Ugandan sides of the Virunga Mountains the gorilla tourism business is still thriving. Moreover, Zaïre has developed opportunities to watch eastern lowland gorillas in its Kahuzi-Biega Park where the animals are so used to people that they can be approached within a metre or two. However, since real cognoscenti say that since the walking is much easier and the lowland gorilla less rare the visitor experience is marginally less satisfying. Uganda has developed mountain gorilla watching since 1993 in Bwindi Forest Reserve (formerly the Impenetrable Forest) where two groups of animals have been habituated by a naturalist. This is part of an estimated $1.5 million donor-funded five-year project to promote tourism in Bwindi as part of the rehabilitation of Uganda's former extensive tourism industry and caters for continued demand to see gorillas in the wild (Harcourt 1980).

Part of the attraction of primate watching seems to be that it is so easy to relate to the behaviour of the animals being watched. This has generated many new, primate-based, visitor attractions and National Parks with almost all generating high quality visitor experiences. Such attractions include the Gombe Stream National Park in Tanzania, set up by Jane Goodall round her chimpanzee research station in 1960

(Goodall 1986). Here visitors can watch chimpanzees from inside caged huts (the cages are to exclude baboons). More recently watching orang-utans has also become popular, in a network of reserves through Sumatra, Borneo and Malaysia. Many have been set up to rehabilitate and release orangs which had been captured for the pet trade. The orang-utan (*Pongo pygmaeus*) was first described by scientists 300 years ago but has since lived in something of a scientific backwater. There are no accurate statistics on its distribution but this seems to be restricted to selected areas of Borneo and Sumatra with probably not more than 20 000 animals left in the wild. A further 900 are kept in zoos throughout the world and there are at least 600 captives in Taiwan alone kept as pets or employed as nightclub attractions. The main threat to the great red ape comes from the pet trade, combined with deforestation. The ultimate survival of the orang-utan is hindered by its slow rate of reproduction (a female may wait nine years between offspring). In addition the attractiveness of babies for the pet trade imperils their survival since the only way to collect a wild baby is to kill its mother. Media exposure of their charms has not helped; orang-utan tourism is boosted each time the Clint Eastwood film *Every Which Way But Loose* and its sequel *Any Which Way You Can* are shown but this also generates volumes of enquiries for pets. The orang-utan population of Borneo is thought to have dropped by 50 per cent in the past 10 years and its survival is not looking good. A baby can fetch 8 million rupiahs (more than £2500) on Jakarta's black market. Any animal older than 3 years cannot be rehabilitated and is irretrievably domesticated (Kavanagh and Bennett 1984). Unfortunately, rehabilitation programmes for orang-utans meet with only limited success and can even further threaten the wild population. Rehabilitated animals can become a bridge between human diseases and wild orang-utans and their reintroduction into the forest can overshoot population carrying capacities. Many rehabilitation centres have become very tourist orientated which reinforces rather than weakens contacts with humans. The Sandakan Sanctuary occupies 43 km^2 of virgin rainforest in Sabeh, Malaysia, and provides a good example. It was started in 1964 to rehabilitate former captive organ-utans and tries to enforce a ban on touching animals within the sanctuary as an effort to prevent the spread of disease. However, visitors are able to interact with mature females outside the boundaries and these animals, touchingly portrayed as being unable to tear themselves away from human company, are actually animals either too old for rehabilitation or where the process was unsuccessful. Visitors to the sanctuary can watch the semi-wild orang-utans come from the forest for their twice daily ration of milk and bananas. Bukit Lawang is also fairly typical. It is located just outside the Leuser National Park in northern Sumatra. Here visitors can climb up to a feeding station where on most days several rehabilitating organs will be receiving supplementary food.

One could argue, however, that despite accusations that this process actually reinforces the bonding with humans the educational value of a visit may in the long run diminish the pet trade. But since the majority of visitors are from overseas and the pet trade is run by local people this seems unlikely. A new approach to rehabilitation is being tried by Herman Rijksen from the Institute for Forestry and Nature Research in Wageningen, Holland, also on a sanctuary along the Kalimantan River. Illegally captured orang-utans are confiscated, quarantined for six months and then held in groups of 10–15 to develop a social structure. They are subsequently released in an area where no wild population exists with supplementary food provided for three months; 90 per cent of the animals disappear into the forest and no longer seek human contact, which probably makes the sanctuary one of the few self-defeating wildlife tourist attractions in the market.

Killing the animals – destructive wildlife tourism

It is tempting to think that wildlife tourism must inevitably be an environmentally friendly activity with minimal adverse impacts. Yet this is not always the case. Sometimes the impacts may be accidental, resulting, perhaps, from poor management or bad visitor behaviour. However, there are several types of tourism and leisure activity which are certainly focused around wildlife but aimed at destruction, rather than conservation. Very often such activities are justified by the participants on the grounds that the species targeted is very plentiful, harmful to humans or effectively being killed for human use. Fortunately, massive organised slaughter, of the type seen in Roman times or Victorian tiger shoots, is no longer a fashionable experience and it is a truism that for tourists the camera has largely replaced the gun. However, a substantial population of visitors to wilderness areas still go there to hunt. This is incompatible with many people's ideal of nature tourism and therefore requires very careful management. Recreational hunting can also be very lucrative and contribute considerable revenues into conservation programmes (as in the Zimbabwe CAMPFIRE programme, p. 93). This is related to the high quality of experience created for participants although many people would question the ethics of deriving high quality experience from destructive activities. These extractive activities can be considered under the following headings:

- foxhunting
- wildfowling
- sportfishing
- poaching
- big-game hunting.

Foxhunting

Despite the view that hunting as a recreational activity is merely organised cruelty foxhunting is still a popular leisure sport and day-trip activity in the UK. It is estimated that as many as 20 000 foxes are killed in the course of a year by the UK's 191 foxhunts, including cubs hunted in the late summer. Hare coursing with beagles, bassets or harriers kills an additional 6000 hares a year and deerhunting with hounds is still permitted in the West Country and the New Forest. Female hinds may be hunted in winter when they are often pregnant or still accompanied by last year's fawn. Badger baiting, outlawed in the 1970s, is still carried on illegally. With that exception these blood sports constitute legitimate recreational activities. However, public opinion favouring a ban on hunting with hounds is at an all-time high. In the UK 150 local councils have already banned hunting on their land and this paves the way for national legislation which will eventually result in a total ban. Arguments stressing the glamorous image of foxhunting, the need to control foxes and the promotion of social cohesion in the countryside no longer carry sufficient weight in the 'green' 1990s. A recent MORI poll suggested that 70 per cent of people would like to see foxhunting banned. Stag hunting with hounds is opposed by 82 per cent of the population and 53 per cent even opposed grouse shooting. Only traditional fishing still received support, with around 12 per cent of people thinking that it should be banned (Vallely 1995).

Wildfowling

Hunters, including supporters of foxhunting, will sometimes argue that they can be considered as active conservationists since they conserve those habitats which support the animals which they wish to kill. In the USA this argument is upheld by the wildfowlers' organisation: Ducks Unlimited bought up breeding marshes to ensure a continual supply of ducks (Wesley 1987). Even conservationists agree that more wildfowl are killed by farmers by competing for agricultural land (as in the case of Canada geese, often considered a pest) than are shot by hunters but it is still doubtful whether this can be justified as a leisure activity. In certain European countries, particularly Italy, there is an annual tradition of shooting small birds, including songbirds, merely for sport. This cannot be justified on any ethical grounds. In the UK birds such as pheasant, partridge and grouse are regularly shot for sport but since such shoots involve birds which have often been initially farm reared and intended for the kitchen at least the outcome is partially justifiable.

Poaching

Poaching, the illegal trapping or killing of wild animals or birds, is a very widespread activity. Within the UK game birds and fish are regularly poached and the USA is currently experiencing tremendous difficulties with illegal poaching in its 366 National Parks. More than 100 species are particularly at risk, including the brown bear, bighorn sheep, elk, grey-banded kingsnake and various species of butterfly. Estimates suggest that at least 3000 American black bears are shot illegally every year, some to supply the black market traffic in animal parts for culinary or medicinal purposes. The size of poaching operations is astounding: 1994 estimates suggest that in the USA alone illegal killing of animals is worth more than $200 million per year, at least half of which goes for medicinal purposes (Van Biema 1994). Some animals such as the hawksbill sea turtle, brown pelican, peregrine falcon and Schaus' swallowtail butterfly are already endangered by hunting or collecting. Despite the huge areas involved (approximately 1.2 million km^2 of parks) only 7200 state and federal wildlife specialists are employed (Yeager and Miller 1986). Such hunting not only endangers species and denies legitimate visitors what they have come to see but has potentially serious long term implications even for relatively common species. Hunters are generally motivated by the desire to obtain a nice trophy to hang on the wall. The most spectacular trophies usually come from large, male animals. This continual hunting of the largest and fittest specimens weakens the common gene pool. Although limited amounts of trophy hunting are allowed in US parks in season (even for species such as bear) off-season hunters are now employing guides or even ordering contract killings for specimens for the wall. A grizzly bear head can be bought for $25 000 without going outside the door.

The wildlife tourism industry of Kenya has survived many crises but one of the most serious was the catastrophic effects of poaching in the early 1980s. Its elephant population, estimated at 130 000 in 1973, was reduced by 88 per cent to 1600 in less than a decade. The rhinoceros population was even more severely affected with Kenya losing 97.5 per cent of its 20 000 rhinoceros leaving a mere 500 by the early 1980s. Estimates suggest that this number will have increased to 680 by 2000. Such a dramatic rise in poaching is the result of a complex of factors stemming from the very rapid increase in human population (to 35 million by 2000) with consequent pressure on land and resources.

Poaching has also dramatically reduced the world's tiger population to the point where tourists will be unlikely to see a tiger in the wild for more than the next few years (McNeely 1988, Myers 1972, Sindiyo and Pertet 1984). India has 60 per cent of the world's remaining tigers in its 21 reserves which form part of Project Tiger but park authorities are unable to control poaching. Tiger tourism has now been quietly dropped from brochures of several nature tourism companies as none are left in many of the Project Tiger reserves and at present captive-bred individuals cannot be returned to the wild. At Nagarahole National Park in India, for example, there are an officially estimated 50 tigers (in practice probably far fewer) which require 250 guards to protect them from the 6000 local people living in villages immediately outside the park who have sound financial reasons for poaching. This is only one example – throughout Asia tigers everywhere have succumbed to poaching and the pressure of human population growth causing a population decline of 95 per cent to the current estimate of 5000–7500 left. By the end of this century it is likely that perhaps 200 tigers will remain, all in captivity (Sutton 1990). Despite the urging of CITES that China and Taiwan, the principal countries involved in the trade in tiger parts, should be subject to economic or political sanctions, little has been done. Poaching has contributed to the probable extinction of the giant panda (*Ailuropoda melanoleuca*). In 1993 the Worldwide Fund for Nature (WWF) who used the panda on its logo admitted that it probably cannot be saved; 800 are thought to remain in the remote forests of south western China, isolated by logging and threatened by poachers. The panda is doomed unless the Chinese government implements a £34 million programme to protect its 12 panda reserves and create 13 new ones linked by 'bamboo corridors'. This plan was announced in 1990 but is still held up by bureaucracy. Meanwhile the best-known panda reserve at Wolong is unable to construct facilities for its visitors and has inadequate security. A lone veterinary surgeon administers the only captive breeding programme which has produced just three cubs in nine years. Poachers trapping pandas by accident have halved Wolong's population in the last 20 years, a process helped by the selling of panda pelts for up to £7000 despite the execution of two dealers in 1990. The giant panda, which drew huge crowds to London Zoo in the 1970s, will soon survive only in zoos, it seems.

Big-game hunting

Unlike India the great National Parks of Africa sometimes have an excess of predators and it is argued that culling (killing) 'spare' predators is a legitimate means of control. Certainly it can be very profitable (see below, p. 95) and have considerable community benefits. Culling surplus animals for profit by big-game hunting has a long history – epitomised in the film *Out of Africa* which preconditioned so many visitor expectations of an African safari holiday. Local people do not hunt for sport; they hunt (or poach) either to obtain meat for food or to kill a predator or sell a product. Today's western hunters shooting for sport form only a small minority of safari tourists but have to be segregated from ecotourists in order to maximise the experience of both. An example of the way this is done is provided by Namibia whose network of privately owned game ranches is expanding rapidly. Potential visitors to game ranches are warned if the ranch encourages hunting and hunters are generally segregated from wildlife watchers. Trophy and game hunting is a highly controlled activity in Namibia and only a relatively small proportion (17 per cent) of the thriving guest farms specialise in hunting although the overwhelming majority (78 per cent) still have suitable facilities (Table 4.2). Hunting is controlled by the Professional Game Hunters Association and the Trophy and Game Hunting Organisation whose members claim high professional standards, meticulously enforced. The Ministry of Wildlife, Conservation and Tourism has been actively supporting farmers who wish to diversify into stocking exotica (species not currently living wild on their land) on the principle that sustainable management increases the possibility of successfully increasing game numbers. The Ministry has a game capture department which sells game to farms if the farmer can obtain a permit.

Table 4.2 Structure of the guest farm sector in Namibia

Type	No.	Ungraded	One-star	Two-star	Three-star	Hunting facilities	Garage	Swimming pool	Discount
Guest farms	45	7	4	24	10	78%	65%	71%	16%
Hunting farms	9	2	1	6	0	100%	78%	78%	0
Totals	54	9	5	30	10				

Permit checks are detailed and include a full environmental analysis, checks on waterholes, fences and ground conditions and an estimate of the carrying capacity for each species. If all is satisfactory the farmer is issued with a permit for a certain number of exotic species and the process is repeated each year. If the farmer is a member of the appropriate professional hunting organisation he or she is permitted to allow trophy hunters to operate on the land under his or her guidance. Such business is extremely profitable as the fees are high and the farmer may earn additional revenue from serving as a guide or taxidermist. Namibia's guest farms probably produce in excess of £3 million a year in revenue, not including extra meals, drinks and services (Shackley 1993).

Throughout the world hunters are prepared to pay high prices for high quality experiences, even if these experiences have potentially disastrous environmental consequences. In Egypt's Sinai Desert, for example, many species including the cheetah and Nubian ass are close to being wiped out by high technology hunters from the wealthy Gulf states. Until recently such hunting was a legitimate activity (it has now been officially banned by President Mubarak) although this ban has been opposed by the tourism ministry. Arab hunters are using night-vision rifle scopes and radar in Sinai and in just one province more than 1000 rare white gazelles have been killed in the last five years – a species already wiped out by hunting in the hunters' home states. Stories abound of emirs hiring or buying entire game reserves to shoot particular species – the brother of one Arabian prince took 70 cars and more than 200 servants on such a hunt.

Sportfishing

All forms of fishing are extremely popular leisure activities although not all are destructive. Fly fishing for salmon, for example, is justified as merely harvesting animals for food. Within the UK fish keeping is a popular hobby and angling a popular sport. Conflicting scientific evidence about the amount of pain felt by fish fuels protests by activists opposed to coarse fishing, a popular leisure pastime where fish are caught and thrown back. In some tropical areas (such as the waters south of Florida in the USA) the increased popularity of sportfishing for large species such as marlin or shark has created pressure on the fish stocks to the point where legislation is being contemplated which would ban trophy fishing and insist that a quota system was enforced.

For its proponents sport hunting or fishing undeniable provides a high quality of experience but it is debatable whether such destruction is morally or ethically justifiable. There are often hidden conservation implications. Sport hunting can reduce the size of an animal population making it vulnerable to tourist pressures. Visitors themselves, in the course of maximising their own satisfaction, can complete the process. The tiny and highly endangered Key deer (*Odocoileus virginianus clavium*) is found only on Big Pine Key some 30 miles north of Key West in Florida. Its numbers were down to less than 50 animals in the 1940s as a result of uncontrolled hunting. The establishment of a National Key Deer Refuge in 1957 has meant that the present population has reached 250–300. The deer's main problems are tourists who visit the area, either to see the deer themselves or to fish and dive. The tiny attractive deer are often seen by the roadside where motorists hand-feed them and take their photograph. Hand-fed deer lose their fear of people and are attracted to highways where they are killed. Moreover, supplementing their diet with unnatural food may affect behaviour and attracts deer to areas where accidents like harassment, dog attacks or entanglement in wire are more likely. Legislation to protect the deer includes strictly enforced speed limits and signs posted showing the deerkill for the year. Generally by the time the first fawns appear in April this may be 20 deer but still tourists feed the animals, gaining a quality experience at the expense of a life.

Questions

1 What factors contribute to the high quality of experience of visitors watching gorillas in the wild?
2 Outline the factors which may influence the satisfaction levels of tourists taking a wildlife-watching holiday.
3 How can the high satisfaction levels of visitors to Etosha National Park (Namibia) be maintained if visitor numbers increase significantly?
4 Do you think that tourism which involves the destruction of wildlife is ever ethically permissible?

5
Wildlife and local communities

One of the clearest things to emerge from two decades of debate about managing the interface of tourism and conservation has been that the success of any project depends on local community participation. In order to ensure maximum benefits for visitor and visited alike local people have to be involved both in strategic planning and subsequent management, and have to develop a perspective which values wildlife as an economic resource. This is easier said than done. Designating an area as a reserve or National Park may frequently conflict with traditional resource management practices meaning that, for example, local people may find themselves excluded from traditional hunting territories. Areas which have formerly provided communities with resources such as grazing or construction materials may suddenly become unavailable and any management plan has to take into account the provision of an alternative resource base, as well as potential compensation. The development of a sustainable ecotourism project should mean financial benefits for local people but this is not always the case. It is often said that the prime function of protected areas in developing countries is to conserve endangered ecosystems for the benefit of the conscience of the developed world. It is certainly much easier to find examples where such tourism benefits tour operators and governments (and, arguably, animals) than it is to see schemes which involve and benefit local people.

Designating an area as 'protected' and giving it some legal status is only one way to conserve its wildlife population. Other ways might include legislation which protects individual species anywhere in the world or captive breeding and return programmes. Protecting an entire area clearly does more than just providing sanctuary to an endangered species: it preserves an entire habitat range (or ranges) which may include numerous distinct ecosystems, and it provides a framework and guidelines for managing this area for the mutual benefit of visited and visitors. Unfortunately, the usefulness of designating a protected area is only as good as the policing and management of that area. An example can be seen in the heavily forested Virunga Mountains of Central Africa which are not only a protected area but a UNESCO-designated Natural World Heritage Site spread over three countries. However, civil unrest has meant that at the time of writing the forest is being cut down at a rate of 1000 tonnes of firewood each day to supply refugee camps so that the forest boundary has retreated 1 mile (1.6 km) in less than two years. Endangered species, including the mountain gorillas, are now being extensively poached for food.

Establishing a protected area for the benefit of endangered species which will also benefit local communities can happen in a number of ways. These include:

- pressure from individuals, sometimes landowners
- private charitable or commercial organisations
- grassroots pressure from indigenous people
- direct intervention by central government.

The bottom-up method with projects initiated at a local level is always more successful, if professionally managed, and generally results in more widely disseminated benefits. We can examine some examples of this process at different scales.

Individual and indigenous efforts

Powerful individuals within a community can make major efforts to conserve and display wildlife. In Ecuador, for example, a native Waorani Indian Caento Padilla became politically active and lobbied the Ecuadorian government on behalf of his tribe. This resulted in the award, in 1982, of land title establishing a Waorani Rainforest Animal Protectorate Reserve in the rainforest basin south of Quito. Caento has formed a tour organisation utilising fellow Waorani as guides to explain the complex ecology of the area, especially the role of small, wild cat species and the function of monkeys, fruit bats and other mammals in pollination and seed dispersal within the forest area. Before the project began the Waorani complained that the animal population was declining (helped by high levels of hunting). Caento restocked the reserve with indigenous species including tamarins, six varieties of monkey, three- and two-toed sloths, toucans, macaws, parrots and many rodents, snakes and small wild cats. An education programme was started to convince the Waorani of the importance of sustaining animal popula- tions in the face of external pressures on the rainforest from road development. New agricultural projects replaced slash and burn and provided a substitute protein source to replace bush meat. Cash income comes from ecotourism which also provides some employment – an excellent example of an individual initiative expanding into a community project.

Similar small reserves established by local co-operatives may be found throughout the world, and are often developed for, and resourced by, ecotourism. In Belize, a small country which receives less than 200 000 visitors a year, a community sanctuary was established in 1985 to protect one of the few, healthy, black howler monkey populations left in Central America. These monkeys, known locally as baboons, are an endangered species found only in Belize, southern Mexico and some parts of Guatemala. Their loud rasping howl can be heard through the forest for over a mile. Howlers live in small troops of 4–8 and during the day they travel through the canopy feeding and resting. Their sanctuary is a voluntary programme dependent on the co-operation of private landlords which has become one of Belize's principal tourist attractions. Most landowners within the 18 square miles (47 km^2) of the designated sanctuary area have signed pledges signalling their commitment to make their farming practices work in unison with the needs of the monkeys and other wildlife so that habitat is preserved (Lindberg and Enriquez 1994).

A similar story can be seen further south in the rainforest of the Tambopata River at the edge of the Amazon Basin in Peru. Here eight species of colourful macaws are abundant in the tropical forest. There are a total of 16 species found in Central and South America of which nine are endangered, mostly by export of rainforest birds for the pet trade. Until the late 1980s it was still quite legal to import wild tropical birds into most of the USA. In this remote area local Machinguenga Indians would occasionally shoot them for meat if they could not get spider monkey or tapir and the bird's habitat was also threatened by gold mining and commercial timber cutting. The Machinguengas are developing a fledgling ecotourism industry based around the conservation of the macaws and their habitat (Munn 1994). This development has recently led to the Peruvian government proposing to construct a 1.8 million acre (730 000 hectares) National Park in the Tambopata-Candama Reserved Zone. It is likely to be popular, especially with current levels of interest in birdwatching (see p. 54), and the elegant, noisy, photogenic and spectacular birds will become Peru's rainforest ambassadors. The system will work by a combination of business and community interests. A new Tambopata research centre has been mostly financed by the Lima brewery and Rainforest Expeditions, a company created by wildlife biologists to take tourists to macaws. Rainforest Expeditions is working with local Indians who have agreed to stop hunting and capturing macaws and help biologists locate the birds in return for radios, money for boats, medicine, education and advice on running Machinguenga's tourist bungalows on Concha Salvador Lake.

Such bottom-up approaches are providing genuine opportunities for sustainable development and the forging of partnerships between commercial and conservation interests. This is not usually the case if the impetus for establishing a protected area comes from government, rather than the local community. The following case study contrasts the above examples with Tortuguero National Park in Costa Rica established by government policy (Place 1988, 1989).

Community impact of Tortuguero National Park, Costa Rica

More than 20 per cent of Costa Rican territory is occupied by National Parks but relatively little data is available concerning their socioeconomic impact on local people. Park construction inevitably means that communities can no longer have access to certain sets of basic natural resources (farmland, wood, game) and the park is likely to have considerable social impact as a result of tourism-initiated development pressures. In 1988 a study by Place examined the relationship between the development of Tortuguero National Park and the nearby Tortuguero village to see how local communities had benefited from wildlife tourism. She found that

Tortuguero National Park, Costa Rica (*continued*)

there had been a general decline in the village's standard of living since the park's construction in 1977, with the increase in nature tourism partially offsetting a decline in commercial resource exploitation. Tortuguero was created to protect the major western Caribbean nesting beaches of the endangered migratory sea turtle *Chelonia mydas*. The park (Figure 5.1) includes 30 km of beach and 20 000 hectares of adjoining forested land. Before its construction local people had made a living from subsistence farming and eating turtle meat and eggs, with hard cash obtained from selling captive turtles and turtle eggs. Both these activities and the trade in selling skins declined after the passing of world legislation to protect endangered species.

The isolated village of Tortuguero contained 27 households but few were self-sufficient in food or other resources. Some villagers had previously owned farms in the park area which were bought out. Nature tourism now provides the villagers with their cash income, replacing the selling of skins or game. Since this began dietary changes have been observed among the population. They ate less meat, game or turtle and instead of being virtually self-sufficient they needed to generate a cash income in order to purchase, rather than grow, food. Despite park regulations forbidding the practice game wardens allowed some turtles to be killed in the summer for food. Although the park did provide employment this was seldom full time and usually with poor pay and conditions. Most local people were in informal employment with few receiving a regular salary. The major employers were researchers, their assistants and tourists staying at a local lodge together with visitors to a fishing camp managed by the government. However, employment was irregular and highly seasonal with a peak in June–mid September when many women were employed as domestics. Extra cash was obtained from visitor spending on drinks or at the local Saturday night dance but the people complained of price rises and a drop in their standard of living.

Who is benefiting from wildlife tourism in Tortuguero? The turtles have gained protection but at what human cost? Tortuguero

Tortuguero National Park, Costa Rica (*continued*)

Figure 5.1 The village of Tortuguero and environs (bottom) and the protected wildlands of north eastern Costa Rica (top)

Tortuguero National Park, Costa Rica (*continued*)

is a remote area where the greatest threat to the turtles was from local villagers who killed a few more than they needed. Incoming tour operators and tourists benefit from the park but on the whole the village has incurred costs, rather than benefits. In this and all similar projects the key to ensuring that local people benefit from tourism based on rare biological or cultural resources has been to involve them from the beginning.

There is much room here for local enterprise with appropriate training and capital. Why are the people not selling snacks, renting canoes, taking visitors on trips? Because they are primarily farmers with no entrepreneurial tradition. Nor are they receiving equal benefits – most tourist cash went to one of the four families who operated a local cafe or lodge. Substantial economic leakages existed as international visitors payed their bills to travel agents in San Jose. Little financial reward was therefore available to local people except quite small wages and tips, insufficient to allow them to accumulate capital to take advantage of potential opportunities. Although there is a lot of potential here for village development projects, it is hardly surprising that at present the people think they were probably better off before the park.

Tortaguero presents just one example of difficult management issues affecting local communities who are being constrained by the lack of opportunities provided for them. There is no simple overall solution as each community is governed by a different set of constraints. Take the case of the Kodiak bears and Alutiiq people of Alaska. Their island off the southern coast of Alaska contains the world's greatest concentration of Kodiak brown bears (one per 1.5 square mile (3.9 km^2), or a total of 2700 on an island less than 100 miles (160 km) long). In 1971 the Alaska Native Claims Settlement Act gave large portions of prime bear habitat to the native Alutiiq people. However, in order to become self-sufficient they would have to develop their land, thus destroying the bears. Current information suggests that the Alutiiq are going to solve the problem by selling the land back to the government to create a larger bear reserve which will generate cash revenue through eco-tourism. However, this seems unlikely to be as reliable a source of sustainable income in the long term as the proposed development programmes, but is the only way that humans and wildlife could co-exist.

There are some cases where humans are co-existing, unhappily, with forms of wildlife which are actively destroying indigenous species. Australia, for example, has a notoriously poor record in wildlife management and is losing mammal species faster than the rest of the world combined. This is largely due to introduced predators such as foxes and cats but several small scale projects have now been set up to establish protected areas, doubling as visitor attractions. At the Warranwong Reserve, half an hour from Adelaide, all such intrusive animals and exotic plants have been removed by the owner, John Walmsley, who is trying to recreate the native bush, not only by eliminating intruders but by restocking with native fauna and flora now including a rare breeding colony of platypus. Warranwong was originally run as a small private reserve admitting 12 visitors per day for either a dawn or nocturnal guided walk at a cost of $10. It won numerous small business and tourism awards and has now been expanded into a holding company, Earth Sanctuaries Ltd, which is developing two additional sanctuaries. In 1993 the group's income was estimated at US$ 6 million. One million dollars have been spent in 1993 to buy more land, build a platypus habitat with three underwater observatories and put up simple guest accommodation. The first sanctuary now has a 14 km fence around it eliminating feral animals from 4500 acres (1820 hectares). New moves for the group include developing three gorges in the Flinders Ranges of south Australia which have a rapidly declining population of 200 yellow-footed rock wallabies. Walmsley, who takes a leading role in all these developments, is convinced that Earth Sanctuaries is an example of the private sector succeeding where the public sector is failing, and he could be right.

Charities and companies

Not all individuals have the ability to construct so ambitious a scheme as Earth Sanctuaries Ltd, nor are they always working in areas where large visitor numbers, relatively straightforward legal formalities and excellent communications and infrastructure would make this a possibility. However, increasingly large numbers of people are becoming voluntarily involved in wildlife conservation and management programmes related to tourism or holiday activities. There are now many commercial organisations which involve participants in 'working holidays' where they can feel that they have made a genuine contribution to the survival of a species or ecosystem, rather than just marvelling at it. In some less reputable cases these ideas are being used merely as marketing devices but there are many examples where positive contributions are being made. The organisation Raleigh International, for example, mounts expedition projects which attract young people wishing to make a lengthy constructive commitment to a single country. This often takes place in the 'gap' year between school and university, or after graduation. Participation is not cheap: a three-month expedition previewed by a short training period will cost several thousand pounds. In the process of raising funds for the project the individual also raises local consciousness about the issues concerned. Many of the projects are development and wildlife orientated. More than 100 members went to Zimbabwe in 1994 in groups of 12–14 working on environmental and community projects although one 'adventurous activity' was added. Some were helping the Department of Parks and Wildlife Management to construct artificial waterholes around Hwange to keep elephants within park boundaries. Others were assisting the wardens of Gonarezhous National Park in the extreme north east of the country with monitoring the results of recent drought before the park could be rehabilitated and reopened to the public. Other projects included field research in the West Nicholson area of southern Zimbabwe where commercial farmers intend to turn 350 000 acres (142 000 hectares) of cattle ranch into an intensive game conservation area. Volunteers have been gathering plant data for the Worldwide Fund for Nature to help to identify the number and densities of game that could be supported.

Large commercial organisations can also become involved in wildlife management with strong community links. The Londolozi Game Reserve on the edge of the huge Kruger National Park in South Africa has three tourist camps along the Sand River. These are part of a network of camps run by The Conservation Corporation which also operates the Phinda Resource Reserve in Maputoland and the Ngala Game Reserve. Ngala was the first commercial partnership agreement between a private enterprise and the Kruger Park, which forms part of the South African National Parks network. The Conservation Corporation is an umbrella organisation which promotes itself as believing in long term commitment to community development based on care of the land, wildlife and people. At Londolozi this is manifested in bush encroachment clearance, repair of erosion and general restoration of the 14 000 hectare reserve to its former productivity. At Phinda there is a habitat restoration programme combined with major restocking including cheetah, lion, hippo, rhino and elephant which are being returned to the area after a 150-year absence produced by overhunting. Community development programmes for staff include a pro-active plan for joint venture partnerships, training in sustainable agriculture, the provision of a market for community produce and the development of a school and clinic. The community work is paid for by the ecotourism clients, most of whom come from Europe. The resorts offer exceptionally luxurious accommodation and services at very high prices, aiming at the luxury end of the wildlife-watching market. New developments include the unique Forest Lodge at Phinda which is almost Japanese in its architectural style. This comprises 16 suites in sand forest, each one glass walled and raised above the forest floor to give visitors the feeling of being integrated with the wilderness. The idea is splendid – but it would be interesting to carry out a detailed study of the economic impact of wildlife tourism on the local communities which might indicate very substantial levels of economic leakage.

Generating and sharing revenue

It is clear in the Tortuguero case study considered above that local people were certainly not receiving their fair share of revenues from nature-based tourism. This is a common problem for indigenous people who live near parks and reserves and who often experience few direct benefits. It is relatively easy to devise schemes whereby this can be improved but very difficult to implement them so that local people share in the revenue. This is especially true for gate fees. When the Kenyan Wildlife Service was established in 1989 by Richard Leakey it began to share out gate receipts within one year (Christ 1994). Initially this had minimal economic impact in the local areas since the fees were so low (US$5) and plans to share up to 25 per cent of the revenue turned out to be overambitious. In 1992 the Kenyan Wildlife Service set up a new Community Wildlife Service and raised gate fees, utilising the principle that tourism revenues generated by wildlife should pay those who bear the burden of co-existing with wildlife. Achieving this goal of community partnership is very difficult in practice but attempts are being made. At Amboseli National Park revenue-sharing schemes are tied in with promoting conservation so that local communities who have experienced problems such as grazing competition, the killing of domestic livestock by wild predators, tick-borne diseases transmitted to cattle and destruction of property can get some recompense. In Kenya it was found that the programmes generated unrealistic expectations without clear revenue-sharing guidelines but in Amboseli they have gradually succeeded in improving local attitudes and reducing the subdivision of land around the park in the buffer zone critical for seasonal migrations. Agreements which are broken can have serious consequences for park management. The Masai of Kenya constantly claimed that outside Amboseli the National Parks authorities did not pay the agreed compensation for cattle losses resulting from lion predation. As a result the Masai poisoned cattle carcasses which killed five lions. A similar problem occurred outside the Masai Mara Reserve where local people resenting the presence of the Kenyan Wildlife Service in the reserve retaliated by killing one of the few remaining rhino.

An additional way of obtaining revenue from wildlife tourism is by carefully controlled hunting. Because of the need to cull overpopulations of animals in parks the idea has developed that limited sport hunting related to culling programmes is ethically defensible and ultimately benefits wildlife and local people. In Zimbabwe the elephant population had grown from an estimated 4000 in 1900 to 50 000 by the late 1980s as a direct result of protection within National Parks. The human population had grown from 0.5 to 7 million during the same period. Drought destroyed trees faster than they could recover from being overgrazed by elephant herds and culling was inevitable, otherwise there would be no environmental recovery. The culling programmes produced meat for protein-starved farmers and the proceeds from the sale of hides and ivory supported conservation programmes. Hostility towards wildlife is not surprising in a country like Zimbabwe where 95 per cent of the population had been forced onto 30 per cent of the land during colonial rule with wildlife given 15–20 per cent.

Culling may not always be the right answer. In the early 1970s the acacia trees of Amboseli were dying and elephant numbers were increasing. Since elephants feed on acacia it was logical to think that the problem was in some way related to overgrazing but in fact the trees were dying as a result of heavy rain which had raised the water table. The soil became very salty and the trees died, with elephants taking advantage of all the extra fodder.

The transition from culling in order to preserve an environmental balance to sport hunting for revenue is difficult to manage and ethically questionable. Kenya banned hunting in 1977 but is now trying to establish a system that permits it but prevents abuses. Hunting is controlled by a network of registered professional hunters under the supervision of the Department of Wildlife and Conservation with clients kept under strict control. Since not all species are endangered quotas are set for more common animals and a high price is charged for hunting them with revenues returned to conservation programmes. Endangered species are never touched. This type of hunting (although repugnant to many) takes very few animals and illegal poaching for trophies poses a much bigger problem. The reasons for the continued popularity of sport hunting are complex; it is an almost exclusively male 'sport' with the trophies symbolising dominance and atavistic instincts. The arguments which justify it say that since people are willing to pay large amounts of money to hunt an animal which needs to be killed anyway to preserve the integrity of a park, there is nothing wrong with setting a high price on its life. The following case study examines an example of where this principle has been applied in practice, with very considerable local benefits.

Zimbabwe – the 'CAMPFIRE' programme linking cash with conservation

Zimbabwe's famous 'CAMPFIRE' (Communal Areas Management Programme for Indigenous Resources) programme started in the Hurungwe district in the north of the country. Local people had problems with elephants damaging crops – one visit can wipe out an entire harvest and there is always the possibility of injury to villagers. The idea behind CAMPFIRE was to enable rural communities to make money from animals which would otherwise be poached because they were pests. It also hoped to encourage an economic development and conservation ethos in rural areas. Before CAMPFIRE communities could not make use of the wildlife on their lands and poaching was common for food or to stop destruction. Now districts accepted into the programme have a quota of animals which may be shot each year for meat or safari trophies. CAMPFIRE is run by the government and conservation organisations and local communities are given a choice either to shoot an animal such as an elephant and sell the meat (which might raise £1600) or to save their quota for safari hunting when the

Zimbabwe – the 'CAMPFIRE' programme (*continued*)

same elephant could earn £4000–6000 for the community. A typical annual wildlife quota per district might include seven elephants, 20 buffalo and 20 baboons. CAMPFIRE created an additional source of income for subsistence farmers. By 1993 eight districts had earned around £35 000 from safari hunting, mostly catering for Americans wanting an elephant trophy. Participating communities must decide whether to invest the money in community projects (schools, dams, etc.) or divide it up for household and personal use. In one ward households earned £60 each on top of their average annual income of £80. The programme also encourages the spread of business skills as local CAMPFIRE committees go into partnership with well-established safari operators to market their quotas and community investments create small scale industries such as beekeeping, grinding mills and tourist ventures. The villagers involved actively discourage wildlife poaching and confiscate snares. It works because everyone involved has to experience tangible benefits so that they feel involved in management decisions. Problems include the fact that animals are nomadic so that an elephant can destroy crops in one area and be harvested for cash in another. There is also no guarantee that a stable annual income will be received, producing considerable pressure to increase quotas. But currently districts are queuing up to be accepted and by the year 2000 more than half the country is expected to be devoted to wildlife conservation under the programme.

All rural development schemes like CAMPFIRE need continual education and training programmes with the eventual aim of creating new means of employment that do not rely on land ownership. This is particularly important in the developing world with high rates of population growth. Many of the benefits that come to local communities from wildlife tourism derive from ecotourism. Other activities include compensation payments, employment in parks and conservation areas and in other sectors of the economy. Ecotourism can also generate revenue to finance the conservation and management of natural areas, usually through entrance fees plus donations or related programmes and this may sometimes (but not always) be sufficient to run the park. Both Bonaire and Saba Marine Parks in the Caribbean charge user fees for diving and the revenue from this plus souvenir sales and donations covers the operating costs. Kenya recently increased park entrance fees from US$5 to US$20 and plans to cover all wildlife management costs through tourism-related revenues (estimated to total US$54 million) by 1995. However, many protected areas charge no fees and in some the fees are too small even to cover the cost of collection (park fees in Costa Rica, for example, stand at US$1.40). Protecting wildlife in an area can be expensive and many parks make a loss even with extensive ecotourism programmes. The Cockscomb Sanctuary in Belize shows ecotourism-related revenues of US$42 213 over a 25-month period but expenditure of US$46 894 over the same time. A new TES/IUCN study shows that only 54 per cent of protected areas in developing countries and 43 per cent in developed countries charge entrance fees. Revenues are returned for use in protected areas by around one-third in both cases so there is clearly some way to go.

People in protected areas

Buffer zones around parks and protected areas are increasingly important in the conservation planning and in creating opportunities to involve local people with management. A buffer zone has use limitations which are intermediate between those of the park and its surrounding area. The term was developed by the UNESCO Man and the Biosphere programme and originally intended to be more restrictive in use than has been possible. Some say the buffer zone policy has failed, others say it has evolved. In Kenya, for example, the savanna National Parks and reserves depend on rangelands just outside the parks for seasonal grazing; 80 per cent of wildlife in Kenya spends at least some time outside protected areas where there are potential conflicts of interest with local people. Outside Amboseli the Masai obtained title to grazing land for the first time and promptly sold it for windfall profits since they were unfamiliar with the 'land title' idea and preferred the cash. Land-hungry farmers bought Masai lands which they fenced and grew crops, excluding wildlife. Rwanda tried the buffer zone idea in its Nyungwe Forest Reserve which was established in 1969 to provide sustainable benefits to people while reducing negative impacts on the park. The Development Through Conservation project imple- mented by CARE in south west Uganda started a small farm extension system around the Bwindi and Mgahinga National Parks which protect mountain gorillas. The project worked closely with mountain gorillas. Both ideas exemplify the buffer zone principle where an area immediately around a park can be sustainably developed for the benefit of local people while at the same time remaining as a resource for park animals.

Buffer zones are often locations for visitor accommodation which can be confined either to a small core zone within the park (as in Etosha, p. 68) or to the buffer zone outside it. This latter solution has the potential to maximise local economic benefits. However, if the park is very large it is impossible to accommodate tourists outside its borders, but visitor facilities located within parks are not necessarily desirable either. The siting of an international hotel in Iguazu Falls National Park in Argentina has caused much criticism although it probably increases the attractiveness of the park to certain types of visitors. There is general agreement among planners that visitor facilities within a park should be low impact and small scale, creating minimal disturbance. Such facilities may be simply on the premise that nature-orientated groups will be happier with more basic facilities which are more environmentally friendly than luxury establishments. The success of the luxury hotels in African National Parks could dispute this view. Developments in many private protected areas are organised by people who are conscious of the potential environmental impacts of tourism. Many consist of small scale facilities preserving the area in a near-natural state while providing maximum economic benefits for local people.

Questions

1 What are the potential disadvantages for local people if their land is incorporated into a protected area?
2 How can commercial firms help local people to earn revenue from wildlife tourism?
3 Refer to the problem of Kodiak bears and the Alutiiq people in Alaska (p. 88). Prepare a feasibility study for the Alutiiq band council evaluating the potential threats and opportunities of developing wildlife tourism on their land.
4 Why do you think the CAMPFIRE programme in Zimbabwe has been so successful? Can you suggest any other countries where similar schemes could be tried?

6
Wildlife in captivity

For many people, taking an expensive wildlife-watching holiday in some exotic destination is not financially possible yet they are still interested in seeing animals at first hand. As we have already seen special-interest wildlife holidays appeal particularly to relatively well-educated people with adequate disposable time and income. The considerable costs involved combined with tiring long haul travel make many such holidays unsuitable for certain market segments, particularly for families with children. Yet it is children that often show great interest in animals and other components of the natural world and desire not only to see them but to find out more about them. If the tourist is unable to visit the animal in its natural habitat then there is only one solution: the animal must come to the tourist. Meeting this need has resulted in the development of a series of visitor attractions based around animals kept in some kind of captivity, ranging from conventional zoos to open-air safari parks.

Some wildlife attractions may aim to display animals to visitors in a close approximation to their natural environment while others segregate them in cages. Most animal-based attractions have conservation-related aims and a strong educational message perhaps aiming to make visitors aware of the plight of a particular animal in the wild. However, not all attractions involving animals are quite so ethically justifiable: many people now object to captive animals being used as performers, such as in a circus, or as unwilling participants in cruel sports such as bullfighting, or bear baiting. Animal rights have now, rightly, become an important issue and the keeping of animals in captivity is regarded by many as ethically indefensible, even if the reason is primarily educational. Other people would argue that a conservation message can be conveyed far more effectively if visitors can see, marvel at and empathise with a living animal rather than just reading about its habits or watching a television programme. Numerous controversies such as these surround the keeping of animals in captivity but we can highlight five major issues which will keep recurring:

- Should animals be kept in captivity, even to educate the public about conservation realities?
- Should animals be taken from the wild to be exhibited to the public or should only captive-bred animals be used?
- Should captive animals be forced or encouraged to provide entertainment for visitors?
- Should there be universal guidelines governing the conditions under which captive animals are kept?
- Is it ethically permissible to finance conservation programmes by exhibiting captive animals to the public?

Types of attractions

There are many different ways to classify such attractions including their:

- objectives (e.g. conservation, education, or entertainment)
- emphasis (e.g. marine environments or specific land mammals)
- level of confinement experienced by the inhabitants (e.g. closed cages or animals allowed to run free)
- species emphasis (e.g. mixed collections or concentration on a single species or ecosystem).

In practice the task of classification is made more difficult by the fact that wildlife-based attractions seldom fall neatly into one category. Many, for example, may have the utilisation of their collections to educate the public as a primary aim but also provide a certain amount of entertainment (perhaps animal rides or animal performances) to get the message through. With the exception of facilities such as aquaria which concentrate on one type of creature, namely fish, most collections are mixed to some degree or another. Even aquaria often have facilities for the display of amphibians or reptiles. Classification by the degree of

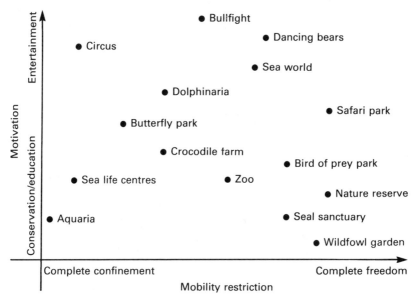

Figure 6.1 Tourist attractions – animals in captivity

freedom experienced by the animal is also difficult as most wildlife-based attractions are mixed with some animals being kept in cages and others, depending on species and available space, being allowed to run free.

Many people think of zoos as the archetypal wildlife attraction although the range indicated in Figure 6.1 is very wide, from conventional zoos to safari parks, butterfly or wildfowl gardens and aquaria. The idea of collecting animals to display to the public has a very long history starting even before Alexander the Great began his famous collection of parrots in the fourth century BC. The modern zoo can be traced back as far as the menageries of Egyptian priests and Chinese emperors and the collections of Montezuma, ruler of the Aztecs, who reputedly employed 300 keepers to look after his animals. Collections of animals seem to be a feature of all civilisations, most commonly used to demonstrate the power of rulers. This could include gifts of rare species from one country to another – a practice which still continues today. Although conventional zoos have always attracted visitors over the past 30 or 40 years the means by which they have done this has radically changed (Blunt 1976, Cherfas 1984). Nowhere is this so obvious as in basic zoo design principles. The greatest revolution in zoo design was produced by the German Carl Hagenbeck who was the first to introduce the park concept of displaying wild animals. This is so familiar to us today that (in the west, at any rate) we no longer expect to see any animal confined in a small, barred cage (Figure 6.2). Hagenbeck's first animal park was opened in 1900 at Stellingen, outside Hamburg, and introduced landscaping, moats and carefully planted trees to give the animals a feeling of freedom. This new idea resulted in the construction of the famous open-plan Mappin terraces at London Zoo to house bears

Figure 6.2 An orang-utan confined in a small cage, Singapore Zoo

and mountain sheep. The terraces were opened in 1913 and closed again 70 years later when they became impossible to maintain. Many of the UK's major zoos operating today follow Hagenbeck's principles – particularly Whipsnade, north of London. This led to the idea of the safari park where animals are allowed to run free and the visitors can drive through their habitat and watch from the comfort of their cars. Many people find this a more acceptable way of displaying wild animals to the public than close confinement in cages.

Whereas 20 years ago most wildlife attractions would have included a wide mixture of species today's zoos and similar attractions often concentrate on just a few. Howlett's Zoo in Kent, UK, specialises in breeding gorillas and tigers. Jersey Zoo, started by the zoologist Gerald Durrell, concentrates on the captive breeding of small endangered mammals with the ultimate objective of reintroducing them to the wild. Individual tourist destinations may exemplify this wide range of choice and different emphasis. A tourist visiting Miami, for example, can choose between four world-famous wildlife attractions:

- Miami Metrozoo (mixed animal collections kept in open environments with an ecological focus)
- Parrot Jungle (exclusively parrots and related species such as macaws, but including performing parrot shows as entertainment)
- Monkey World (exclusively monkeys, kept in an open environment with their visitors kept in cages)
- Miami Seaquarium with huge fishtanks, displays replicating different marine environments, captive dolphins and a rehabilitation centre for injured manatees (sea cows).

Within the UK wildlife-based attractions such as zoos compete as day-trip destinations with heritage attractions, resorts and theme parks. In recent years other nature-based attractions such as rare breed sanctuaries and farm parks have also become popular, especially with children. Although these concentrate on domestic stock many include displays of wild animals. At White Post Modern Farm Centre near Nottingham, for example, visitors are attracted by the opportunity of feeding a wide variety of farm animals, but the farm also includes displays of owls, local wild mammals and a hedgehog rehabilitation centre for specimens injured on the roads.

Some wildlife attractions (such as a seal sanctuary) may focus around a particular species, while others concentrate on a particular issue (perhaps captive breeding of endangered species). Some specialise in land animals while others (including those growing most rapidly in popularity) focus on marine environments displaying fish and aquatic mammals in aquaria and specially constructed displays. This great range is shown diagrammatically in Figure 6.1, although it must be remembered that there may be great variations between different establishments included under the same heading (such as zoos). The attractions shown may include facilities unfamiliar to people based in the UK. Sea World centres (p. 113), for example, are a chain of enormous and lucrative enterprises based around performing marine mammals such as killer whales and dolphins. They differ from the smaller UK-based Sea Life Centres (p. 104) which reconstruct different marine environments with a strong educational message. Other animal attractions such as dancing bears are now only found in Eastern Europe and parts of the Middle East although one could argue that animal-based leisure activities such as cockfighting and badger baiting still found in the UK belong to the same category. Bullfighting is confined to Spain, Portugal and parts of South America. Alligator farms where animals are raised primarily for their meat and hides but also used as visitor attractions are found in some of the southern states of the USA and also crocodile farms in parts of Africa. They may sometimes claim an educational function and also have elements of entertainment such as the alligator wrestling displays of the Florida Everglades (p. 114) but their ultimate aim is commercial, raising the reptiles for meat and hides.

Tourism and wildlife-based attractions

Despite the controversial nature of the above issues the fact remains that many people do still wish to visit animals in captivity though that number is declining. Of the Top 10 wildlife attractions in Table 6.1 only three had not suffered a drop in visitor numbers since the previous year and two of those had no admission charge. Only two zoos appear in the overall view of the UK's 20 most popular tourist attractions indicating that zoos have lost out to alternative destinations for a day trip, particularly heritage attractions and theme parks (Table 6.2). This drop is partly the result of the great proliferation in visitor attractions which has not been matched by a corresponding increase in visitors. The result is that while the number of potential trip-makers remains static and their choice of destinations increases individual destinations need to become increasingly innovative and competitive to retain market share. However, more than 20 million people visited animal-based attractions in the

Table 6.1 1992 visits to wildlife-based attractions in the UK (* indicates estimate)

Attraction type	Number in UK	Approx. no. of visitors (thousands)	Average no. of visitors per attraction (thousands)
1 Zoos	20	4900	244
2 Sea Life Centres	8	2600	321
3 Bird gardens, wildfowl centres	21	2000	95*
4 Safari or zoo parks	3	986	329
5 Nature reserves	11	527	48*
6 Seal/otter sanctuaries etc.	6	508	87
7 Butterfly parks	7	285	41
8 Aquaria	4	145	36
9 Birds of prey centres	2	61	31
10 Misc	28	3100	111*
Totals	110	15 112	134.3

Table 6.2 Zoo visitor survey

When was the last time you visited a zoo or wildlife/safari park?
In the past five years	52%
More than five years ago, but less than 20 years	29%
More than 20 years ago	11%
Never, or can't remember	9%

What was your reason for visiting?
For a day out	48%
To entertain children	40%
To find out more about animals and conservation	6%
To see a new animal, baby animals or a new exhibit	4%
Other reasons	2%

If you could only see one type of animal, which would it be?
Big cats	33%
Apes/monkeys	23%
Penguins/seals	12%
Elephants	9%
Pandas/bears	8%
Other/don't know	15%

What is the most important function of a zoo or wildlife/safari park?
Conservation of endangered species	53%
Education about how animals live	28%
Entertainment	11%
Research into animal behaviour and physiology	7%
None of these is most important	1%

Table 6.2 Zoo visitor survey (*continued*)

What kind of zoo or animal park would you prefer to visit?

Safari park – drive around while animals roam free but can't necessarily get close	69%
Zoo allowing you quite close to animals, but they are in large pens with barriers like walls, moats and ditches	26%
Traditional zoos – can't get close to the animals even if this means small pens or cages	4%
None of these	1%

What most annoyed you on your last visit to a zoo or park?

Not enough space for the animals	25%
Too high an entrance fee	15%
Animals seemed unhappy or disturbed	15%
Not enough information about the animals	10%
Some animals you wanted to see were not on display	9%
Too many people to allow good view of animals	5%
None of these	22%

How do TV and radio wildlife programmes compare with visiting a zoo or animal park?

They help enhance enjoyment of a visit	65%
They're so good they render zoo or park visits unnecessary	21%
However good, they don't replace seeing live animals	12%
Don't know/no opinion	3%

Should zoos be abolished?

No	70%
Yes	27%
Don't know	3%

UK during 1992, over 30 per cent of the total population. More than 7 million of those visits were made to zoos with a further 3.7 million to safari parks. New types of animal-based attractions are continually being developed, the current fashion being for owl and bird of prey centres as well as facilities which concentrate on underwater environments. Nearly 600 000 people visited the Sea Life Centre at Blackpool, part of a trend emphasising public interest in any attraction with a maritime theme. There are now 18 Sea Life Centres in UK coastal tourist towns attracting half a million visitors per year. They are basically aquaria, many specialising in the presentation of local marine environments.

Although visiting captive wildlife is still popular the nature of the attractions being visited has changed in response to the anxieties listed at the start of this chapter. The last 30 years have seen an immense revolution in popular taste. For example, in the late 1950s London Zoo attracted 3 million visitors per year but it now gets less than a third of that figure. Many of the 1950s visitors were coming to be entertained by the chimpanzees' tea party or the possibility of getting a ride on an elephant or camel. Today's visitors want to see animals which have recently featured in television wildlife documentaries or which are especially rare or endangered. Seeing furry baby animals or watching animals being fed is still popular but today's youthful zoo visitor is just as likely to be visiting a tarantula which he or she has adopted or participating in a snake demonstration. The visitor is less likely to be laughing at an animal's behaviour and more likely to be reading an informative display. Today's visitors are better informed, better travelled and far more environmentally aware than their 1950s counterparts. Interestingly, this has not led to the demise of the captive animal attraction but to a great shift in emphasis to cater for changing popular tastes. Attractions such as seal sanctuaries where injured animals are being rehabilitated are guaranteed crowd-pullers whereas strong public feeling now exists against the use of performing animals in circuses, although 30 or 40 years ago performing animals were common, even in zoos. During the 1950s the keeping of performing animals and animals in cages was not such an emotive issue as it is now. Far less was known about the behaviour of animals in the wild and fewer tourists had ever experienced the thrill of seeing a wild animal. Even Butlin's holiday camps featured captive animals as entertainers, sometimes with disastrous results such as the elephant which fell into the swimming pool at Skegness Holiday Camp and drowned. There is a far greater variety of animal-based attractions around today to cater for every taste and moral standpoint. Today's tourists, sophisticated consumers of nature television programmes and heavily influenced by the 'green' policies of the 1990s, are becoming increasingly aware of ethical issues surrounding the keeping of animals in captivity. This has shifted the balance in wildlife-based attractions favouring those which conserve, educate and research over those which merely entertain. Unfortunately, research is expensive and must frequently be financed from visitor admission fees creating a tension within zoological institutions.

Table 6.1 shows that zoos still dominate, although marine attractions and wildfowl centres are becoming increasingly popular. Of the 110 wildlife-based visitor attractions in the UK nearly 30 per cent attract over 100 000 visitors per year to such diverse attractions as Easham

Otter Trust, Long Sutton Butterfly Park, Banham Zoo and Monkey Sanctuary and Bentley Wildfowl Collection.

Conditions of captivity

One of the greatest areas of concern in wildlife-based attractions are the conditions under which the animals are kept. It is necessary to create both the right habitat for visitors and visited, in order that the former may have a good experience and contribute financially to the welfare of the latter. Fashions in animal keeping change as fast as fashions in tourism and practices which might have been acceptable a few decades ago are frowned upon today. Moreover, there is some evidence to suggest that living conditions seen by the visitor as palatial may not necessarily appeal to the animal. Luxurious enclosures and cages may have the function of salving the conscience of the visitor who can convince him- or herself that the animal is better off in captivity than in the wild. This may have a positive spin-off for the visitor attractions which, by exhibiting apparently well-cared-for creatures in well-maintained environments, are therefore able to charge higher prices and create extra areas of visitor spend. Luxurious living conditions can never really act as the sole justification for keeping animals in captivity. The Mirage Hotel and Casino in the desert city of Las Vegas, Nevada (USA), is famous for its breeding population of white tigers which are used in the stage act of magician/illusionists Siegfried and Roy. White tigers come from central Asia, about as far from the Nevadan Desert as it is possible to be, and it could be argued that training them to perform in a nightclub act does not accord with the dignity of the animals. However, the casino owners justify their presence on the grounds that the tigers have a successful breeding programme and appear to be thriving. They stress the expensive air-conditioned quarters used to display selected animals in the casino foyer (on a rotation basis) as evidence for their care and the fact that the animals are apparently happy. The tigers are undeniably successful as tourist attractions, pulling visitors into the casino and supporting one of the longest-running and successful cabaret acts in the history of the city. But is it morally right to keep them in captivity, primarily for human entertainment?

The luxurious tiger accommodation at the Mirage is the exception, not the rule. Although zoos and similar institutions have their animal accommodation closely monitored there is cause for concern about the living quarters of some circus animals, for example. When they are not performing many circus animals, including big cats, are often housed in small, ramshackle, metal container lorries ('beast wagons'). Elephants remain shackled in tents with other animals such as zebras, camels and llamas and horses are tied up in bare stalls during the nine months of the year while the circus is travelling. The International Association for the Welfare of Animals (IAWA) keeps a close watch over the more than 20 circuses in the UK who still use animal acts and supports the growing trend towards animal-free circuses. The use of animals in circus acts is unjustifiable for a number of reasons, including:

- poor living conditions for animals
- circus acts trivialise animals
- most circus animals are still captured from the wild
- visitors do not particularly like animal acts.

Training is hard for a wild animal such as an elephant with strong natural instincts and behaviour patterns and circus animals are often mentally damaged by captivity stress. They begin to exhibit the stereotypic behaviour once seen in zoos: tigers and other big cats pacing their cages, elephants waving their heads from side to side. Fortunately the era of animal performers has to be coming to an end, especially when recent research suggests that children (the prime customers for a circus visit) actually prefer clowns and trapeze artists to performing animals. A number of UK animal-based circuses have actually closed in recent years including Blackpool Tower Circus which closed in 1989 after 84 years. However, despite concerns over the health and welfare of circus animals and a feeling that no circus can provide an acceptable way for animals to live, there is still some room for doubt over the precise effects. An animal psychologist commissioned by the RSPCA to look at circus animals in the UK concluded that many enjoyed their training and performance and that their acts were no less dignified than showjumping, dog racing or cat shows. But the public certainly seems to be voting with its feet.

Inevitably, keeping captive animals is an expensive business. The more luxurious the accommodation the more expensive it is to construct and maintain, but in the case of endangered species their accommodation simply has to be funded. In the future some animals will survive in captive breeding programmes even when they are extinct elsewhere. The science writer Jeremy Cherfas once estimated that by the year 2000 there will be only 750 Siberian tigers left in the world and they will all be in zoos since the species will have become extinct in the wild. Their food, maintenance and veterinary bills will cost US$ 2.5 million US per year (Cherfas 1984). Most of this money has to be recouped from zoo visitors, who are usually motivated more by the desire to have a good day out rather than by a burning interest in conservation. This means that in order to attract adequate funding from visitors the modern zoo needs to entertain, as well as to inform, creating an inevitable dilemma (p. 98). This gap can be partly bridged by innovative methods of keeping and displaying animals.

The greatest advances in zoo management and display techniques have taken place in North America where new collections of animals have often been able to be housed on large sites which permit technological innovation, rather than the cramped urban zoological gardens of Western Europe. Being unhampered by the weight of tradition has enabled zoos in North America to innovate in ways that would be impossible at, say, London Zoo (see below, p. 116). New ways of exhibiting collections are being devised to replace the traditional taxonomic methods where all members of the same family such as cats (Felidae) or horses (Equidiae) are displayed in the same area. Larger spaces have enabled species to be organised in regional or ecological groupings and encouraged the visitor to understand how the different animals actually live together in the wild. Toronto Metro Zoo was the first to be arranged on this regional principle and is spread over a huge 285 hectare site with four main pavilions. The African pavilion includes two sets of environments, jungle and swamp, where animals from different habitats can be seen in a close approximation to their natural habitat. Objections to this kind of display sometimes come from keepers (the displays are much more difficult to manage) and also from environmentalists who say that there is little evidence to suggest that they alter the quality of life of the animal and may merely constitute window dressing and salve the conscience of the visitor. Do animals prefer these fake environments? Visitors certainly do. Such displays are inevitably very expensive both to construct and maintain, but they are also most attractive. At the wonderful Antarctic exhibition at San Diego Zoo visitors can enjoy the $7 million Penguin Encounter, a huge, icy, mock polar environment of 465 m^2 with specially cooled and filtered air and lighting mimicking polar climates. Visitors can gain a feel of what the arctic is like in a way that could not be replicated by seeing penguins round a stagnant pool. A moving walkway transports visitors and the design also permits the six resident species of penguins to be viewed underwater. Purists say that not all the penguin species in the display would naturally belong in the wild but something must be right as the exhibit is not only aesthetically pleasing but has a successful captive breeding programme. San Diego was proud of breeding the first emperor penguins to hatch in captivity. Is this all merely set dressing to make the visitor feel good? Penguins are unlikely to be fooled by their expensive hi-tech environment but visitors might develop an interest in penguin conservation as a result of the dramatic display.

Very little is known about the impact of visitors on captive wildlife although some negative interactions are well known. This includes the bad publicity given on the very rare occasions when a member of the public is injured on a visit to such an attraction, inevitably through their own fault and despite comprehensive security procedures. There have been cases of determined visitors climbing into lion and tiger enclosures or across high walls to reach gorillas, sometimes with fatal consequences. Other, less severe, visitor impacts include:

- feeding of animals with wrong foods
- deliberately teasing and disturbing animals
- effect of visitor noise
- effect of artificial lighting.

Wildlife attractions try to address these issues by developing regulations and clear signposting informing visitors what behaviour is acceptable and what the effects on the animal might be. This has to be supported by adequate policing (by keepers) or simply making access to the animals impossible. Illegal feeding of animals is a particular problem, particularly with animals such as elephants which not only beg for food but charm visitors with the way in which such tips are received. Signs are often posted informing visitors what the animal's normal diet is and how sick it will become if fed the wrong food. In the case of certain species at open-plan attractions the visitor is encouraged to buy the correct food and hand-feed certain animals which generates extra profit for the attraction and ensures that the animal is fed correctly. Other issues, such as the effect of noise and light, have been quite poorly researched and the assumption is often made that if the animal exhibits no distress and breeds satisfactorily then its quality of life must be adequate.

The public is often more concerned about the living conditions of higher mammals kept in captivity but there is evidence to suggest that many creatures, including fish, do experience stress from visitors. Although the keeping of fish in captivity does not raise the emotive issues presented by marine mammals there is plenty of evidence for negative visitor interactions. Flashbulbs are apparently particularly distressing to fish in aquaria. This problem is felt most acutely in Japan which has more than a hundred large aquaria attracting huge crowds of camera-wielding visitors each year. Fish frightened by the endlessly popping flashlights crash fatally into aquaria walls; one exhibit lost 1500 fish in this way (half the original population) during its first six months after opening.

Public concern over aquaria is particularly intense where marine mammals such as killer whales or dolphins are being kept in captivity. These concerns also extend to the origin of the animals and only recently the otherwise admirable Vancouver Aquarium received a bad press for the live trapping of Arctic beluga whales for its displays. Officials argued that the beluga was one of the commonest varieties of whale and that the captive populations were a valuable study resource. However, anyone who has visited the beluga exhibit cannot but be shocked by the small enclosures as well as surprised by the apparent interest which the whales display in their visitors. Conservation organisations such as Greenpeace and animal welfare groups are concerned about the welfare of such captive marine mammals – particularly when they are kept in locations considerably distant from the sea. Despite the obvious constriction of life in a relatively small tank for animals accustomed to the open ocean aquarium keepers have been heard to argue that there is no scientific evidence to suggest any reason why killer whales and dolphins need water more than 10 m deep. This would remove the argument that confining large marine mammals in small tanks is cruel.

There is also the problem of captive animals escaping from zoos and other attractions. In late 1993 Bill the Bison escaped from the American Adventure Theme Park near Derby causing a danger to pedestrians. Bill, weighing 1.5 tons (1.52 tonnes), was being delivered from Chester Zoo where he had been born and grown up. He was part of an advance party of four buffalo (the remaining eight were to follow) destined to occupy a 22 acre (9 hectare) corral as part of a themed Wild West exhibit. Fortunately Bill was recovered unharmed despite fears for the safety of passing pedestrians.

Educating the visitor

As we have just said the aquarium is probably the least controversial means of keeping wild creatures in captivity as the public seems to think that fish are inherently less aware of their restricted surroundings. This may account for the fact that over the last decade aquaria have become popular visitor attractions as part of a generally increased level of interest in anything to do with marine environments. An aquarium is basically a series of tanks with fish, sometimes supplemented by 'touch pools' or exhibits featuring marine mammals or birds such as seals, dolphins or penguins. It is seldom justifiable on conservation grounds and sometimes largely stocked (and frequently restocked) from the wild which may deplete natural fish stocks. However, aquaria certainly perform a valuable educational function introducing tourists to a set of environments which, unlike terrestrial ecosystems, very few of them will ever be able to see. They vary from simple facilities to large and technologically complex establishments with multi-million-dollar start-up costs. The best aquaria such as the magnificent facility at Monterey in California are committed to education and conservation programmes and frequently include important ecological research programmes and the breeding of rare and endangered species. The worst are nothing more than a series of gloomy fish tanks, sometimes poorly maintained. However, compared with zoos aquaria do little captive breeding and their constant need for new tropical fish may deplete wild stocks. Other aquatic facilities such as seal sanctuaries combine education with the rehabilitation of sick or injured animals. Some may be very successful indeed. The National Aquarium in Baltimore, Maryland, was opened in 1987 and owned and largely paid for by the city of Baltimore as a focus for an urban renewal scheme. It has been outstandingly successful and led to the development of the Inner Harbor as one of the east coast's major visitor attractions. An economic impact study suggested that within three years of opening it had created 3000 jobs and generated some $88 million in tourism revenues. A major $35 million extension was opened in 1990 to house marine mammals.

Entertaining the visitor

Throughout the world there are many outstanding wildlife-based attractions which successfully combine the provision of high quality living conditions for their inhabitants with a strong educational message. This includes the innovative African savanna exhibit at Seattle Zoo which pioneered the idea of combining animals which would naturally be found in the same environment together in a single exhibit. Other facilities such as the 'gorillaria' at Howlett's and Port Lympne Zoos in the UK which specialise in breeding endangered apes try to keep both visitor and visited entertained, in order to raise the quality of both sets of experience. A common way of doing this is called 'behavioural enrichment', where an animal is encouraged by a stimulus to perform some activity closely related to what it would do in the wild (Markowitz 1982). This has three vital functions:

- the animal does not become bored
- visitors are entertained and educated at the same time
- the animal is able to obtain exercise.

At Howlett's the gorillas are fed from the top of their enormous wire mesh enclosure with the result that they must continually forage to pick up their food. This is a behaviour pattern that they would follow in the wild and it means that the animals are constantly active (although they have unlimited access to quiet sleeping quarters) with plenty for visitors to watch. Another idea, followed in many wildlife attractions, is to make this kind of activity interactive where the visitor plays a role in stimulating the animal. A typical exhibit might involve the visitor pressing a button which releases food and stimulates some small animal to emerge from its hiding place. The visitor gains the satisfaction of feeding the animal, which entertains its visitor and is rewarded with food and encouraged to take exercise, At Zurich Zoo visitors enjoy watching chimpanzees utilise twigs to fish for food inside artificial mounds using techniques that in the wild they would use to obtain termites. The bear compound at Copenhagen has a tree from which honey flows at certain times, encouraging the bears to climb the tree and entertain the visitor.

Although it is relatively easy to invent ways by which bears, for example, can entertain their visitors this is more difficult in the case of animals such as fish which are quite boring to watch. Innovations in aquarium management have included such things as giant tanks big enough for divers to enter, combining maintenance of the exhibit with entertainment for visitors. At Miami Seaquarium, for example, divers in the largest tanks use cleaning equipment and feed fish while maintaining, through an intercom system, a commentary which both entertains and informs the visitors. Some animals are fortunately natural clowns – the charming, furry sea otters at Vancouver entertain visitors with their antics which makes them a popular exhibit – cost effective even though each otter costs an estimated £5000 per year to feed, requiring a gourmet menu including crab, calamari and clams.

There can be few ethical objections to animals performing natural food-gathering functions which also happen to entertain visitors but there is a very fine line between this type of behavioural enrichment and what happens in wildlife facilities where the primary aim has changed from education/conservation to entertainment. This may involve encouraging animals to act as 'clowns' or to take part in spectacles which some visitors consider demeaning. Sea World centres in the USA are theme parks based around marine mammal displays, offering perform-ances which have much in common with those of a circus. Captive killer whales perform in six 'shows' per day in high season in addition to trained dolphins, seals, sharks and walruses. This is lucrative for the management since the spectacles are very attractive and visitors, often staying 3–4 hours, spend freely on souvenirs, catering and merchandise. There have been many claims that such performances trivialise animals and early shows followed banal scripts which had much in common with the now-extinct 'chimpanzees' tea parties' which attracted visitors to zoos during the 1950s and 1960s. Supporters claim that the dolphins and whales are only taught to use themed tricks which are related to their natural behaviour patterns and that they are simply having a good time with their trainers. They claim that the experience is stress free since it is impossible to force such powerful animals to do anything against their wishes but bizarre displays can be encouraged by providing rewards. Since the killer whales do not breed in captivity and are solitary rather than permitted to live in their natural large social groups the experience cannot be that stress free. The animals are kept in relatively small tanks and often captured from the wild especially for performances. Few would support the argument that such practices are justified by the claim that watching such performances stimulates interest in the species which eventually contributes money for conservation. If captive marine mammals are so happy how come the average life span of a captive dolphin is 10 years in captivity and 35 years in the wild? Killer whales have the same natural life span but average two years and seven months in captivity.

Many animal rights supporters would also feel unable to visit a nightclub act or a circus where animals perform 'tricks' to entertain tourists, but clearly not everybody feels the same way or such acts would not exist. There is very little difference between animals kept for circus acts and those utilised in cruel sports such as bear baiting, badger baiting and cockfighting. The first two of these involve animals captured from the wild and killed in a particularly repulsive manner. Dancing bears are still tourist attractions in eastern Mediterranean countries such as Greece and Turkey, used as begging aids to extract money from visitors. The organisation Libearty has undertaken to rescue many of these bears and set up a sanctuary programme, although the sanctuary itself has recently been criticised as inadequate. Many captive bears are still caught from the wild and tortured to develop behaviour patterns such as 'dancing' which entertains tourists. Captive semi-wild bulls are used in bullfighting which is often justified as a celebration of the spirit of the Spanish-speaking world. Happily, bullfighting has steadily diminishing appeal as a tourist attraction. Revelations that claimed increases in humane precautions such as protection for the picadors' horses are actually ineffective have dented the popularity of the sport and animal rights activists are concerned that the horses themselves (right at the end of their working life) still run a strong risk of being gored or disembowelled and are kept in very poor conditions.

Nor is bullfighting the only example of this kind of tourist-orientated entertainment. Seminole Indians 'wrestle' alligators on the Tamiami Trail in the Everglades near Miami for the entertainment of tourists. Although these reptiles are technically not wild they are certainly not domesticated either. The creatures, although bred in captivity, are often kept in cramped conditions and after a lifetime of being gazed at they end their days as crocodile burgers and the raw materials of handbags. Such alligator and crocodile farms are common in tropical areas from South America to West Africa although the spectator sport is confined to the US southern states. Alligator wrestling is quite safe for the human (though uncomfortable for the alligator) since the muscles which open and close an alligator's mouth are relatively weak and to take a bite from a human the alligator must thrash its head from side to side. This looks spectacular but actually the human can open and shut the animal's jaws to order. The continued popularity of this 'sport' must relate to the spectator perceiving a wrestler to be in danger and, like observers of motor racing, just waiting for the wrestler to make a fatal mistake.

The role of the modern zoo

Today's zoo must function as a stationary ark performing a series of complex and often conflicting functions such as:

• conserving endangered species
• educating people about animals

- safeguarding the welfare of visitors
- entertaining visitors to generate revenue
- providing visitor facilities such as catering and merchandising
- breeding animals to halt decline in the wild
- reintroducing captive-bred animals into the wild
- carrying out zoological and veterinary research to improve animal welfare in the wild and in captivity.

Conservation and captive breeding is an enormously expensive business and in order to fund such activities a zoo must be able to raise cash. The most obvious way to do this is from visitors. Each zoo's stock of animals is listed under the ISIS system (ISIS is the International Species Inventory System) based at Minnesota Zoo outside Minneapolis. This computerised register helps organise breeding programmes and the development of species survival plans but most of this expensive though vital conservation and research work is carried out unknown to the average zoo visitor. Campaigners against zoos often point out that of around 10 000 zoos world-wide only 1200 are registered for captive breeding and wildlife conservation and that only 2 per cent of the world's 5926 threatened species are registered in zoo breeding programmes. Of these programmes a mere 16 projects have successfully returned animals to the wild. This is a disgracefully small fraction of the estimated 5 million animals confined in zoos, most simply there to provide human entertainment.

The zoo visitor survey, the results of which are summarised in Table 6.2, confirmed that visitors preferred seeing animals in safari park situations rather than in cages and that this was particularly important for young visitors (aged 15–24). But not all zoos have the space to exhibit their animals in this way and such facilities are enormously expensive to run. Lack of space for animals was the biggest cause of complaint closely followed by worries that animals seemed unhappy or disturbed. Visitors also wanted more information about the animals, reinforcing the educational value of such a visit. Only 21 per cent of people thought that television made zoo visiting unnecessary and 65 per cent thought that such programmes enhanced the pleasure of a zoo visit. Overall, 70 per cent of people were in favour of keeping zoos, across all age groups and regional divides. But the high costs involved and difficult ethical issues have brought several major zoos near to closure, as is discussed in the following case study.

Saving London Zoo

London Zoo, hamstrung by past weaknesses, underinvestment and amateur management, was declared extinct on 17 June 1992. Since that time its fortunes have turned round. How has this been achieved?

The Zoological Society of London was founded in the 19th century by Sir Stamford Raffles and Sir Humphry Davy to study zoology 'with animals as objects of scientific research, not of vulgar admiration'. This statement underlies many of its current problems in maintaining a balance between education and entertainment at a time of diminishing resources. The Society's Regent's Park Zoo opened to visitors on 27 April 1828 with barred cages, signs warning of dangerous animals and little effort to cater for visitors. Its visitation peaked in the summer of 1950 when the birth of Brumas, a baby polar bear cub, attracted 3 million visitors. Since then it has been downhill all the way.

In 1992 the Department of National Heritage axed the zoo's grant on the ground that keeping animals on a 37 acre (15 hectare) site in central London was no longer appropriate. No managerial agreements could be reached about the proper direction to take and the zoo was preparing to close, yet by October 1993 it had its first working profit for 17 years. What saved the zoo? Dr Joe Gipps, its current Director, attributes the turnaround partly to the Emir of Kuwait who gave the zoo £1 million as a gesture of thanks for British action during the Gulf War. In addition the publicity generated by the zoo's problems brought the potential closure of a major national attraction to the attention of the general public and this resulted in a huge increase in gate receipts. Joe Gipps successfully reversed 20 years of poorly directed management which had reduced annual visitation from 3 million to less than 850 000. The reasons for the decline are complex and not all internal. Over the last 30 years there has been a vast increase in the number of rival day-trip attractions, especially those providing competition for the attention of today's sophisticated child consumers who might prefer the London Dungeon to a ride on an elephant. Waste, incompetent management and a desire to be all things to all men increased the zoo's problems. Its urban location

Saving London Zoo (*continued*)

cannot be significant since Berlin Zoo, also an urban zoo, gets 2 million visitors a year. In the past development has been hampered by listed buildings such as the once-famous Mappin Terraces where conservation protection prevented improvement.

Joe Gipps' business plan involves costs of £21 million over a 10-year reconstruction programme including redesigning the aquarium and converting the Parrot House into Invertebrate World. Many animals have already been dispersed to other zoos. A popular television documentary series charted the reorganisation of the zoo and also boosted awareness of the different research programmes and the issues under debate. The zoo opened a new £1 million children's zoo area in August 1994 based around a touch paddock featuring pets and domestic animals plus reindeer and camels. The emphasis is very much on conservation and education and the area was privately financed by an Italian businessman in memory of his daughter.

An advertising campaign promoting the zoo's work with the captive breeding of endangered species also did wonders for its image. It seems likely that London Zoo will survive as a small, specialised, particularly British institution focused on conservation and research without either the room or the resources to follow San Diego or Seattle – which is, ironically, exactly what its founders intended.

Does a zoo really give its visitors a better understanding of animals? Is this better than they could obtain by seeing animals in the wild or watching them on film, video or in virtual reality? The future of zoos seems to indicate a polarisation between two different categories of zoo. At one extreme there will be small zoos which contain relatively few species presented in a natural environment with a great deal of visitor information. At the other extreme there will be larger zoos with a wider range of species and the emphasis on reconstructing environments utilising high technology. All zoos will need to demonstrate good scientific research and breeding programmes and it will no longer be sufficient for any wildlife-based attraction just to house animals, or to utilise them as entertainment.

Questions

1 Do you think that technological innovations such as virtual reality and interactive television will ever make zoo visiting redundant?
2 Do you think that the primary job of a wildlife attraction is to entertain or to educate the public?
3 What methods are used by wildlife-based attractions to generate revenue from visitors for conservation and captive breeding programmes?
4 'Capturing whales and dolphins for aquaria is justifiable since it stimulates public interest and eventually produces money for conservation.' Do you agree with this statement?

7
Management, protection and value

Wildlife-based tourism is a non-consumptive way of utilising wildlife resources to benefit human populations. If properly managed it can offer a country the chance to develop a high value-added industry that simultaneously offers protection by either removing or reducing the incentives to exploit wildlife or develop land for alternative purposes such as agriculture (Barnes *et al.* 1992).

As we have already seen the growth of interest in wildlife-based tourism over the last decade has been phenomenal and greatly outstripped most planners' calculations. This is a trend set to continue; a recent market survey by the Costa Rican Tourism Institute anticipates a 300 per cent increase in natural-history-based tourism by the year AD 2000. Costa Rica also exemplifies another positive trend – increasing volumes of domestic tourism related to concern and publicity about wildlife and conservation issues. Until recently wildlife tourism was very much the preserve of relatively wealthy and leisured travellers from developed countries. The change is welcome, although it increases the strain on natural resources within protected areas. Visitor entries to Costa Rica's parks are now (officially) 10 times the volume of 1980 when they stood at a modest 1500–3000 per year. Current official figures exceed a quarter of a million but in practice may be 30 per cent higher. Few countries collect adequate statistics to measure volumes of wildlife-based tourism at park, regional or national level despite the fact that this is essential for effective marketing, planning and prioritising improvements in services. In Dominica, for example, there are no entry gates or park guards and thus no entry figures (Weaver 1991). In cases where records are kept these may be very inadequate, as in the case of the Galapagos (below, p. 132). If no statistics are kept then it is almost impossible to measure the impact of tourists in protected areas and generate effective management plans.

Many South American countries, especially Belize, Dominica and Ecuador have seen dramatically increased volumes of nature-based tourism over the past few years. All have substantial areas of protected land at different stages of development for wildlife tourism. Countries such as Mexico, which receives more than 5 million visitors per year, are developing new wildlife products and visitor attractions such as the Monarch Butterfly Reserve in Michoacan, a seasonal attraction where visitors can marvel at millions of butterflies overwintering from North America. This market expansion and product diversification raises issues of how we value and price wildlife (below, p. 126) within a general framework of the management of protected areas. Policies vary a great deal between countries. Belize, for example, has a policy of promoting small scale sustainable developments which theoretically benefit local people, although this does not seem to be working in practice. Recent estimates suggest that up to 90 per cent of coastal developments in Belize are under foreign control. Visitors to these hotels take day trips into nature reserves producing resource utilisation patterns quite different from those of committed, long stay, environmentally aware ecotourists. Erlet Cater, a specialist in the study of tourism in developing countries, noted that while the designation of National Parks and reserves may meet the needs of conservationists and, if properly managed, those of present and future tourists, the prospects for sustainable development of the host population may be compromised. Despite the claims that ecotourism is more environmentally sensitive as the numbers of ecotourists increase they create the same demands on infrastructure as conventional tourists. As national prosperity increases so does the propensity to take day trips and all five countries listed above are having problems managing the major regional impacts caused by these new developments (Cater 1992). Parks such as Iguazu Falls in Brazil/Argentina now get more than 2 million visitors per year, most from nearby cities.

We can therefore summarise these introductory remarks by emphasising that wildlife tourism is not only a rapidly developing industry but one that is undergoing considerable internal shifts, notably an increase in domestic tourism. Management issues within this framework include:

- the need to obtain reliable data to form the basis of development plans
- ways of estimating the economic and social value of wildlife
- understanding the need for protected areas to conserve wildlife and act as foci for wildlife tourism development.

The acquisition of reliable data is a fundamental necessity in any management planning for wildlife tourism. It can help managers to identify resource conflicts, determine their objectives, calculate the costs and benefits of wildlife tourism and fit such tourism into its national and regional context. Extensive literature is available to guide those who are engaged in the production of such plans, mostly produced by IUCN and UNEP (e.g. Salm and Clark 1984, MacKinnon and MacKinnon 1986, WTO/UNEP 1992). A fundamental need is for basic visitor information to help in the preparation of budgets and capacity calculations. These are usually based on entry statistics and surveys of visitor origin and arrival mode, combined with geographical studies of travel patterns and preferred visitor activities at the wildlife tourism destination (viewing, camping, walking, fishing, education, etc.). Such data helps us establish any potential areas of resource conflict and devise methods of protection for especially fragile or outstanding sites.

Valuing wildlife tourism

Most of us would be able to list the potential economic benefits of developing wildlife tourism, which could include:

- generation of direct and indirect employment opportunities
- stimulation of domestic industries (catering, transport, guides, souvenirs)
- production of foreign exchange
- diversification of a local economy especially in rural areas
- creation of demand for local agricultural produce
- stimulation of improvements to local transport and communications
- productive non-consumptive use of marginal lands
- facilitating the development of conservation and recreation programmes.

However, many countries are only just beginning to promote nature tourism to protected areas and most national plans still focus on traditional tourism. Developing wildlife tourism needs co-operation; it cannot be left to the Wildlife or National Parks services and needs integration between tour operators and governments. National organisations such as Parks services are inevitably (and correctly) conservation orientated but in order to derive revenue from visitors it is necessary to utilise their resources in order to develop and sustain a wildlife tourism product which visitors will want to buy. As we have seen, a common financial problem in developing countries is that tourism revenues are not returned to either tourism development and marketing or to assisting in the management of protected areas (Abala 1987).

Economic impact calculations require good statistics and unless these are available the results will be biased and unreliable. Despite the existence of umbrella organisations such as the World Travel and Tourism Council (WTTC) and World Tourism Organisation (WTO) standard information is not available and there is minimal co-ordination with conservation organisations such as IUCN (the World Conservation Union). Global economic estimates of the value of nature tourism vary from a few million to over a trillion US dollars and are arrived at by multiplying estimates of general tourism by the percentage of general tourism that nature tourism represents. In 1994 the WTTC estimate is $US 3.4 trillion in gross output (sales) with a WTO estimate that 7 per cent of this results from nature tourism, giving an estimate of $US 238 billion for 1994. These figures are open to debate.

Wildlife tourism can provide economic justification for areas that otherwise might not get protected. In Rwanda, for example, the mountain gorillas were not only the third largest source of foreign exchange for the country but their protection required habitat conservation and prevented deforestation in a country which had Africa's highest population density. Surprisingly little is known about the economic impact of visitors to protected areas although it is widely thought that nature-orientated visitors spend more than more 'conventional' tourists. The 1988 WWF airport survey (p. 59) suggested that nature tourists spent less time than conventional tourists in a country but more money (the Galapagos or Rwanda are good examples here). But it is still uncertain how much of these revenues remain in the country as many are paid out to home-based tour operators. In extreme cases local visitor expenditure may be little more than permit fees, guides, drinks, tips and souvenirs which form a very small proportion of the several thousand pounds paid for the holiday. The main local benefits are often employment generated by tourism although this may be seasonal and erratic (p. 87). Studies done of the value of a specific park or protected area to the regional or local economy generally use methodologies to justify the park's existence from an economic standpoint. Local economic statistics are site specific and easier to research.

Some macroeconomic statistics are available to give us an idea of the size of the industry. Residents of the USA, for example, spend $4 billion annually on wildlife viewing trips (Robinson and Bolen 1989, Shaw and Mangun 1994) plus $600 million on field guides, bird houses, bird baths in 1980 (including $500 million per year just on bird seed). We can also price individual destinations or products. Kaza (1982) estimated conservatively that the whale-watching industry of California, based around observation of the grey whale, attracted 235 000 whale watchers in 1981 and was worth $2.2 million. Tilt (1987) made a similar calculation for the whale-watching industry across the USA estimating that it attracted 1.5 million visitors per year and was worth $25 million in fares alone, plus land transport meals and lodging totalling around $1 billion per year. It seems probable that 15 years later this value can be doubled. More detailed microeconomic studies of wildlife tourism utilise methods such as travel cost (Knetsch 1963) and survey or contingent value (Davis 1964). Other work has been survey based. Wesley (1987) discussed a survey of 1882 randomly selected members of Ducks Unlimited, the wildfowling and conservation organisation (above, p. 76) which estimated their personal waterfowling expenditures on equipment and supplies. This indicated that the organisation probably generates annual expenditure in excess of $1 billion, with $100 million of that on annual expenses for members who, on average, hunted less than 10 days or more each year. Such figures did not take into account expenses on travel, food, accommodation, ammunition and incidental costs.

Entrance fees are a major method of gaining revenue from wildlife but in many areas they are both inadequate and insufficient to allow a park to generate sufficient income to become self-supporting (Baldares and Laarman 1990). A flat rise in an entrance fee could create problems with domestic tourists (who generally have less overall disposable income than international visitors). Since a protected area is part of any country's national heritage the only workable solution is a two-tier entrance fee for non-residents and residents, often with a third tier admitting local people from buffer zone areas completely free. Such a scheme is often adopted for cultural sites as well. Some studies of visitors and entry charges have produced surprising results. One piece of work carried out in Nairobi National Park (Abala 1987) suggested that people's willingness to pay to visit the park was significantly affected by congestion but quite unrelated to the presence of animals.

Price control of visitor numbers – the Kenyan National Parks

In Kenya, tourism employs 8 per cent of the labour force. Development has largely depended on external donors and funding agencies such as the World Bank which traditionally have been wary of tourism projects. Despite the fact that Kenya contains more than 50 parks and reserves the vast majority of visitors go to well-known and accessible areas such as the Masai Mara, Amboseli, Samburu, Tsavo and Lake Nakuru which are very overcrowded. Indeed, the central circuit of Amboseli has been reduced to nearly a semi-desert by visitors. The Kenyan Wildlife Service plans to combat this problem by instituting a series of new visitor management strategies. These include limiting access by carrying out more research on park carrying capacities to establish firm quantitative limits on the numbers of vehicles entering the park each day. This raises the cost to users as access to the most popular sites becomes regulated by price and ability to pay. Such a resource management method stands open to the charge of elitism but it is difficult to see a viable alternative. A supplementary price control method is making differential charges for certain circuits within heavily used parks. A highly desirable route would have a higher price than one which takes the tourist to a less frequented area. This method requires the installation of modern technologies at entry gates combined with detailed monitoring of visitor behaviour to make sure that everyone is keeping to the rules.

By making a larger amount of areas within National Parks available to the visitor the carrying capacity of a park such as Amboseli can be greatly increased (possibly up to as many as 10 million visitors per year). However, this requires very considerable capital investment to open up new areas which in practice will only be accessible by air because of the distances involved. The necessary infrastructure includes roads, accommodation and visitor

The Kenyan National Parks (*continued*)

centres but could encourage forms of tourism with high per capita revenue and low environmental impact. The traditional vehicle-based wildlife watching has drastic environmental consequences, as we have already seen. Introducing a wider range of special-interest activities such as camping, walking, climbing, bird safaris, fishing, and camel or horse safaris in designated areas would attract a wider range of visitors but disseminate their impact more widely.

In order for such programmes to work effectively there would need to be financial compensation to park residents and more sharing of gate receipts (see p. 91). These could be increased by price rises and supplementary price controls such as the use of a fixed voucher system which would either cover the whole of a visitor's stay in Kenya (allowing unlimited access to all parks) or be valid just for selected parks. Leakage of revenue from park gates is a problem which could be partly solved by a season ticket system or a system of central ticket sales. Some differential pricing is inevitable, both to stimulate domestic tourism and allow local people to visit the park and to develop off-season tourism. Increased revenue could also come from renegotiating the terms of leases for lodges within the parks and possible nationalisation of the lodge and hotel system, although at present this would be impossible to finance.

Since the publication of this plan in 1991 which, it was hoped, would aid in increasing tourism to Kenya by 10 per cent per annum during a five-year period (as well as providing substantial resources for conservation) other factors have intruded. International finance was not so readily available as had been hoped and in 1992 there was a 20 per cent drop in visitors as a result of media coverage of robberies in parks and poaching of animals. This increased management costs as more armed guards were employed together with necessary aerial monitoring and surveys. The bottom line would appear to be that if the ideas are successful tourism to Kenya's most popular areas will become more expensive and more exclusive, reinitiating a life cycle of product development which started with the 1930s safaris.

If demand exceeds supply then gate prices will inevitably rise and can be used as a market regulator. Differential pricing merely refines this approach. In the case of Kenya visiting coastal resorts (such as Mombasa) will eventually become cheaper for the visitor than going to National Parks (despite the 1993 introduction of a $2 bed tax to fund environmental and safety improvements). The role and personality of the head of the Kenyan Wildlife Service is also crucial here and in January 1994 Richard Leakey resigned in response to a campaign accusing him of arrogance and racism although it seems possible that he had uncovered corruption and exorbitant salaries. His defenders, who included the World Bank, tour operators and environmentalists, pointed out that since his appointment in 1990 the KWS had obtained more than $300 million in loans from international donors for an 8–10-year period and that annual revenues have increased tenfold. Since his resignation there are reports that elephant poaching, which had virtually stopped as a result of staff increases to more than 4000 well-armed men, has restarted and there are increased worries about tourist security. Unless his successor can reverse this diminished confidence it is not impossible that big donors like the World Bank and EC might freeze millions of funds causing the implementation of wildlife tourism and development planning to come to a halt.

Pricing and valuing wildlife

The arguments surrounding placing economic values on wildlife are complicated by different ethical and religious attitudes towards the environment. Placing a monetary value on wildlife to ensure its survival is a dangerous game (Eltringham 1984) since if such an economic argument fails then there is no justification for saving the wildlife. The ecological value of non-resources (e.g. inconspicuous but not endangered species) cannot be calculated. This inevitably means that they are undervalued within their ecological context as we may lack knowledge of the role some species play in their ecosystem and the potential of such species as human resources. Many people would argue that wildlife should be conserved regardless of its measurable economic worth, and that it is the duty of governments to enforce this by enacting and enforcing legislation.

Calculating the value of an individual resource (or species) is contentious. Most of the calculations have been done in connection with hunting or other extractive activities. We can get a simple game species value by dividing the money spent by hunters per species by the number of animals killed. Norman *et al.* (1976) estimated, on this basis, a value of $11 200 per bighorn sheep, $6400 per black bear, $20.79 per blue grouse and $1.21 per muskrat in a North American context. We can also get such an estimate by assessing the annual income that the landowner receives from such hunting. Eltringham (1984) showed that it cost £20 to produce a single red deer for hunting on infertile lands in Scotland yielding profits of only around £1.25 per hectare. However, the land was unsuitable for any other purpose.

To summarise, the various methods available to measure the economic benefits of wildlife are:

- calculating total gate or licence fees to estimate the value of tourism in a particular destination
- estimating visitor expenditure on equipment, lodging, food and transport within a designated area
- looking at employment generated.

It is very difficult to establish an economic value for animals yet such a calculation is important when wildlife conservation policies are based on the premise that the price which a tourist will pay to see an animal is greater than the value of that animal as meat or hides. In Amboseli (Kenya) an attempt was made to estimate the value of living animals of different species. An individual lion was thought to be worth US$27 000 per year in tourism revenues while the entire elephant herd was priced at $610 000 (Thresher 1981). These calculations were based just on viewing rather than hunting or other consumptive activities. The bottom-line figures estimated the park's net value for wildlife viewing at $40 per hectare and compared this with agriculture where even the most productive activities would only earn US$0.80 per hectare. A further study in 1972 calculated that developing the park's wildlife ör tourists could produce an annual income 18 times as great as the area's value in beef production, assuming that both industries were working at maximum capacity. This kind of calculation is relatively easy to do for large, well-known, African game animals in areas where visitor figures are known and alternative uses are available. But how do you price the worth of a butterfly in Mexico or the elusive jaguar in the rainforests of Belize?

Some cost–benefit analyses have been done in National Parks but few with much emphasis on wildlife. In the Virgin Islands National Park

(VINP) the calculation involved direct costs (operation and maintenance) and indirect costs (including interest on federal investment in VINP properties and taxes lost on properties removed from local government control). The measure of direct benefits was the effect of the VINP and its concessionaires in the local economy plus indirect benefits from impact on the island's boat industry and intangibles such as increased land values. The total benefit/cost ratio worked out at 11.1/1 making the park a sound economic proposition. However, this kind of economic data is very thin on the ground. It has also been argued that emphasising the economic value of parks would lead to decision-making processes whose outcomes were determined on profit rather than conservation criteria. Thus if a park protecting an endangered species failed to make a profit it would, on this theory, be reasonable to replace it with another economic activity such as agriculture or ranching.

We should also consider whether a wildlife resource can have educational value, as well as social and economic value. It is possible to obtain an educational value, for example, by looking at the number of student visitors, their age range and institutions and asking what significance the species or areas have in local education. We could also count the number of researchers entering a protected area and the publications which they produce, assessing the contribution of the area to research and scholarship. Social value (calculated as the percentage of a local population visiting the area) is easy to estimate if the arrivals statistics are accurate but less easy to determine its significance. Wildlife may be of quite unquantifiable value in the aesthetic or spiritual significance to a community, with its survival having philosophical as well as ecological implications. We have already seen (above, p. 62) that many visitors considered seeing gorillas in the wild as a spiritual experience. This idea has now been enshrined by the IUCN (1990) which says protected areas are for 'inspirational, educative, cultural and recreative purposes'.

Designating protected areas

Tourism is only one of the issues concerning managers of protected areas, who need to achieve a balance between the needs of humans and those of wildlife. Other concerns may include:

- conserving endangered species
- controlling predators

- preventing the introduction of exotic species
- dealing with species overabundance
- determining responses of wildlife to human visitors
- managing migration and seasonal fluctuations
- avoiding humanly caused disease and diseases transmitted from human to animals and vice versa
- managing extraction
- establishing values for wildlife.

Of course many of these issues impinge on tourism. Conserving endangered species may produce a visitor attraction, such as the bison at Wood Buffalo National Park in Canada. We have already encountered the problems of transmitting diseases from visitors to wildlife in the context of mountain gorillas, who contract colds, measles and hookworm. In the present day concerns are being expressed about the diseases which humans can contract from wildlife, particularly exotic fevers such as Lassa fever and (possibly) AIDS from tropical primates.

Sustainable development on a global scale requires part of the earth to be set aside as protected areas, in order to conserve the environmental and cultural heritage for the enjoyment of all people and to ensure ecological balance as the nation's population increases. Unfortunately, the upkeep of protected areas is very expensive and must generally be recouped by promotion of tourism. Over 130 countries do not have protected areas, totalling more than 5 per cent of the world's land surface, but each system varies according to needs, priorities and levels of legislative, institutional and financial support. IUCN has defined a system of protected area categories as follows:

I Scientific Reserve/Strict Nature Reserve (undisturbed except for scientific study)
II National Park (large area, no commercial extractive use, of outstanding natural and scenic significance)
III Natural Monument/Natural Landmark (small area focused on protection of specific features)
IV Managed Nature Reserve/Wildlife Sanctuary (protecting nationally significant natural landscapes while providing opportunities for recreation and tourism)
V Protected Landscape (nationally significant landscape)
VI Resource Reserve (protected for future use and to prevent development)

VII Natural Biotic Area/Anthropological Reserve (to allow a way of life in harmony with environment to continue undisturbed)
VIII Multiple Use Management Area/Managed Resource (nature conservation orientated towards the support of economic activities).

Two further categories are also used, namely:

IX Biosphere Reserve (as designated by the UNEP Man and the Biosphere programme in the 1970s, which conserves significant entire ecosystems to safeguard genetic diversity) and
X World Heritage Sites (to protect both natural and culture features of outstanding global significance).

The IUCN scheme for assessing the suitable protection category is shown in Table 7.1. We can see that major wildlife tourism resources are included in most categories (Table 7.2).

The management of wildlife tourism is inextricably connected with managing protected areas, since the existence of such protected areas stimulates tourism (Budowski 1976). Creating park management plans for tourism is very expensive and often can only be afforded in a developing country where international funds are available. Such a plan may not be updated very frequently even if there are substantial changes in the type of tourism or in other local conditions. In parks where the priority is tourism a good management plan includes the provision of visitor facilities, staff and their training and the development of roads or trails. Visitor education programmes are necessary and guidelines must be laid down for integration with local communities to help develop growth strategies. The most frequent problem encountered involves increased flows of visitors which greatly exceed original estimates, stressing the park's infrastructure and its plant and animal communities. Although this kind of stress is often quoted there is very little quantitative evidence and some is anecdotal. Such problems can only be controlled if there are the resources available. Increased visitation to the Galapagos Islands, both a World Heritage Site and a Biosphere Reserve (Table 7.1), caused environmental impacts such as behaviour changes in albatross and sea lion populations, observed by local communities, but this was controlled by strong preventive measures. The following case study examines some of these points in detail (Broadus and Gaines 1987, de Groot 1983, Emory 1988, Kenchington 1989)

Management, protection and value   131

Table 7.1 Simplified scheme for assessing suitable protection category

				Recommended status	IUCN category
Protection of nature highest priority	Visitor use disturbing or of low priority	Visitor use and active management undesirable	Primarily for preservation	Strict Nature Reserve	I
			Primarily for research	Scientific Reserve	I
		Zoned visitor use and/or some management desirable	Biologically valuable	Managed Nature Reserve	IV
			Geophysically or biologically spectacular	Natural Monument	III
	Visitor use high priority	Not for consumptive use	Global priority	World Heritage Site	X
			National priority	National Park	II
			Local priority	Provincial Park	II
		Consumptive uses for local people	Global interest	Biosphere Reserve	IX
			Regional interest	Anthropological Reserve	VII
Protection of nature secondary priority	Water catchment vital	High visitor potential		Protective Recreation Forest	VIII
		Low visitor potential		Hydrological Protection Forest	VIII
	Water catchment not vital	Hunting or harvesting value high	Hunting a priority	Hunting Reserve	VIII
			Traditional use a priority	Wildlife Management Zone	VIII
		Hunting or harvesting value low	Essentially natural	Agro-forestry Reserve	VIII
			Essentially agricultural	Protected Landscape	V

Source: MacKinnon and MacKinnon (1986)

Table 7.2 Protected areas and wildlife tourism destinations

Protected area category		Wildlife tourism destination
I	Strict Nature Reserve	Gombe Stream National Park (Tanzania) (chimpanzees)
II	National Park	Etosha National Park (Namibia) Iguazu Falls (Argentina/Brazil)
III	Natural Monument or Landmark	Angkor Wat (Cambodia)
IV	Managed Wildlife Sanctuary	Manas Wildlife Sanctuary (Peru)
V	Protected Landscapes	English National Parks
VI	Resource Reserve	Brazil's Forest Reserves
VII	Anthropological Reserve/Biotic Area	Central Kalahari Game Sanctuary
VIII	Managed Resource Area	Ngorongoro Conservation Area (Tanzania)

Tourism in the Galapagos Islands

The Galapagos consists of a chain of 19 volcanic islands, 97 per cent of which have no human settlement. It became famous as a result of Charles Darwin's visit on the *Beagle* in 1835 and is one of the world's major ecotourism destinations where 90 per cent of the reptiles, 50 per cent of the land birds and 45 per cent of higher plants are found nowhere else. Indeed, for many people visiting the Galapagos equates to making an environmental pilgrimage. Between 1970 and 1985 the numbers of tourists, mainly foreign naturalists, grew steadily from negligible volumes to about 15 000 per year. By 1987 this had more than doubled to 32 500 following the opening of a second airport in 1986 (Wallace 1993).

The Galapagos Islands are both a World Heritage Site and a Biosphere Reserve; 90 per cent of the land area is part of the National Park, under the jurisdiction of Ecuador. In 1976 the Galapagos National Parks Service and the Charles Darwin Research Station joined forces to control tourism to the islands. It was decided to focus tourism on minimum impact activities relating to nature and the environment and not to support other recreational activities such as watersports. In 1985 a further tourism plan decided that this strategy was too narrow and recommended diversification away from ecology to include diving and watersports but this was rejected and the decision taken to

Tourism in the Galapagos Islands (*continued*)

retain a clear ecological focus, despite very rapid increases in tourist numbers.

Management plans for the Galapagos divide the area into five zones, of which only two are open to visitors; 43 sites have been designated as open to visitors, 25 extensive sites for small groups of up to 15 people and 18 intensive visitor sites. Visitors must stay in tightly controlled groups kept together and supervised to minimise disturbance, with the trained guides stopping visitors from straying from paths. Minor management problems include complaints by visitors who feel overwhelmed by the quantity of information (tourists usually complain of the opposite) and feelings of claustrophobia resulting from never being able to get away from the group. Two categories of guide are utilised. National Parks Guides have a degree in biological science and multi-lingual abilities and can accompany groups of 30 visitors. Auxiliary guides are local residents who have completed a shorter course. Tension exists between the two groups.

Despite concerns about rising levels of tourism in the Galapagos there is little available research examining the specific effects of visitors on animals. Tours to the Galapagos are very readily available, marketed through international agencies with visitor numbers doubling every five years since 1970 and expected shortly to reach 50 000 per year. The numbers are now too great for existing strategies and some Extensive Use sites are showing signs of track erosion. The plan, aimed at controlling international visitation, requires most tourists to be accommodated on boats and enforces strict controls over sites to be visited. This theoretically precludes the development of any substantial land-based infrastructure. It is, however, becoming increasingly inadequate in the face of the expanding number of small scale uncoordinated developments, especially small hotels and guesthouses, which are being constructed to meet the needs of the increasing numbers of Ecuadorian domestic tourists. Such establishments provide considerable economic benefits to the local population. However, the capital, Puerto Ayora Gaql, now has tatty souvenir shops and a human population grown from a few thousand in the early 1960s to

Tourism in the Galapagos Islands (*continued*)

14 000 today as a result of unrestricted immigration when the Galapagos were declared a province of Ecuador. This has put tremendous strain on water resources and the high population has proved a fire hazard.

Official policy is becoming increasingly irrelevant in the face of what is actually happening on the ground. A new policy is needed to cope with these large numbers which must combine a solution for stressed sites with scope for the introduction of new products such as interpretive centres which have considerable educational value but reduce visitation to fragile sites. Procedures need to be designed to enable local residents to gain more benefit from the tourist industry. Other management methods, such as rationing or a price-discrimination scheme to restrain demand while increasing management revenue, have to be considered. The economic benefits to Ecuador could be spread more evenly if tour operators were encouraged to offer joint packages including the Galapagos and the Amazon headwaters of the High Andes, a trend already discernible. However, the issue of environmental impact is not solely related to visitor numbers. Social and economic factors such as increased domestic tourism make an absolute ceiling on tourist numbers impracticable for the foreseeable future. The higher the level of visitation to an area the more likely it is that funding will be sufficient for management plans and ecological studies but the greater the problems created by visitors.

What can we learn from this protected area case study? Firstly, it is clear that many of the problems stem from an inability (or unwillingness) to enforce existing regulations, as well as a marked change in the nature of visitation with a new emphasis on day-tour operations creating management problems. Other points from the introductory list (p. 128) also recur, notably the difficulties experienced in excluding introduced exotic species and the need to develop new visitor sites to spread the load. There is some reason for optimism in the Galapagos: a variety of national and international organisations have provided funds for improvements because of the significance of the park, and there has been a levelling off and slight decline in visitation in the early 1990s

(Wallace 1993) not as a result of diminished interest but of political instability in neighbouring countries. This has provided a breathing space for park management structures to be reassessed. The most obvious lesson learnt is that increases in visitation to a protected area or site must never exceed the management capability to handle them, with a careful balancing of commercial and conservation opportunities operating for the benefit of wildlife, visitors and management.

Endthoughts

It seemed fitting to conclude this book with a case study of perhaps the most significant wildlife tourism attraction in the world and its many problems. This chapter has drawn the readers' attention to the way in which the wildlife tourism market is changing, within a global context. It has also emphasised the difficulty of controlling an industry with such considerable economic potential. Earlier case studies of marine environments noted the threat from increased volumes of diving tourism, yet with tourist-related activities at the Great Barrier Reef increasing six-fold since the early 1980s and earning $90 million each year and Florida's coral reefs alone thought to be worth $1.6 million per year (Eber 1992) is it any wonder that it is difficult to enforce legislation in the face of commercial pressures? It now seems clear that the growing threats to our global environment and the need for sustainable management of limited resources cannot sensibly be met by a move to alternative tourism but rather by changing the way in which mass tourism is conducted. Despite claims that wildlife-based tourism is more environmentally friendly and sustainable there is a great deal of evidence to suggest that as it becomes popular the problems of mass tourism are being replicated. Environmental protection is best achieved by voluntary codes of conduct. There is an Environmental Research Council operating under the WTTC banner which lists more than a hundred partnership agreements and guidelines involving numerous different types of organisation at different scales. But making such agreements work is far more difficult than drawing them up in the first place. Governments see tourism as a highly desirable growth industry which helps diversification and foreign exchange. However, since the market comes to the producer (rather than the other way round) it is therefore relatively unprotected. Undeniably tourism to protected areas often develops in relatively remote peripheral regions where there are few alternative income sources and where it can stimulate growth. The organisation Tourism Concern maintains that the industry has to go beyond cosmetic changes (including 'greenwashing') to consider social issues involved in tourism development projects. These may include the displacement of people from their homes, loss of livelihoods and lack of access to public land. Wildlife tourism, like other facets of the industry, is unpredictable and influenced by factors such as political stability, the weather or international currency fluctuations. While giving the individual tourist a very high quality experience it may cause overcrowding and damage to the resources which have attracted the visitor in the first place. This effect was noted more than 20 years ago and is becoming progressively severe as visitor numbers increase and the consumer cycle requires access to progressively more remote destinations. Nor are these developments without substantial costs to the host country which may not be recouped because of economic leakage. Unexpectedly high levels of tourism to an area may have surprising indirect repercussions on local ecosystems. It would be possible to argue that where the objective of a visit is to see a single species this is far from being a guarantee of the survival of that species, which will be determined by a complex of factors of which wildlife tourism is only a small part. Many people went to India to see tigers but the revenue generated was insufficient to fund the enormous costs of the small armies of guards required to protect the tiger from poachers. Wildlife tourism, therefore, may be incidental to species survival. It is also no guarantee that a protected area will survive and indeed as more visits are made to protected areas increased pressure has highlighted weaknesses in management methods. Many of the adverse impacts of wildlife tourism are both tragic and self-defeating. An area which loses the wildlife which attracted visitors will experience potential economic and environmental catastrophes. This problem is being partly addressed by planning solutions involving the integration of parks and protected areas into entire regional management schemes. As we have seen competition for resources is at the heart of most conflicts between parks and local communities but it can be avoided if local people are allowed to play more significant roles in selecting and managing both protected areas and tourism projects.

Questions

1 What methods are available to enforce conservation regulations in protected areas?

2 In what ways might designating a location as a World Heritage Site assist in conservation and tourism management?

3 Discuss the efficiency of pricing policy as a means of raising revenue from protected areas.

4 Why does an increase in domestic tourism often create problems for protected area managers in the developing world?

Bibliography

Abala, D.O. (1987) A theoretical and empirical investigation of the willingness to pay for recreational services: A case study of Nairobi National Park *Eastern Africa Economic Review* 3(2) 111–119.

Almagor, U. (1990) A tourist's vision quest in an African game reserve *Annals of Tourism Research* 11(3) 31–47.

Ankomah, P.K. and Crompton, J.L. (1990) Unrealized tourism potential: the case of sub-Saharan Africa *Tourism Management* 11(3) 11–27.

Bacon, P.R. (1987) Use of wetlands for tourism in the insular Caribbean *Annals of Tourism Research* 14 104–117.

Baldares, C. and Laarman, J.G. (1990) *User Fees at Protected Areas in Costa Rica* FPEI Working Paper 48, Southeastern Center for Forest Economics Research, North Carolina.

Barnes, J., Burgess, J. and Pearce, D. (1992) Wildlife tourism, pp. 136–152 in Swanson, T.M. and Barbier, E.B. (eds) *Economics for the Wild* London: Earthscan Publications.

Barstow, R. (1986) Nonconsumptive utilization of whales *Ambio* 15(3) 155–163.

Bart, W.M. (1972) A hierarchy among attitudes towards animals *Journal of Environmental Education* 3(4) 4–6.

Blangy, S. and Nielsen, T. (1993) Ecotourism and minimum impact policy *Annals of Tourism Research* 20(2) 357–360.

Blunt, W. (1976) *The Ark in the Park: the zoo in the 19th century* London: Hamish Hamilton.

Boo, E. (1990) *Ecotourism: the Potential and the Pitfalls* Vols 1 and 2, World Wildlife Fund for Nature.

Boullon, R.C. (1985) *Planificacion del Espacio Turistico* Mexico: Edition Trillas.

Boyle, S.A. and Samson, F.B. (1985) Effects of nonconsumptive recreation on wildlife *Wildlife Society Bulletin* 13 110–116.

Broadus, J.M. and Gaines, A.G. (1987) Coastal and marine areas management in the Galapagos Islands *Coastal Management* 15(1) 75–88.

Brown, P.J. (1984) Benefits of outdoor recreation and some ideas for valuing recreation benefits, pp. 209–220 in Peterson, G.L. and Randall, A. (eds) *Valuation of Wildlife Resource Benefits* Boulder, Colo.: Westview Press.

Brown, P.J., Haas, G.E. and Driver, B.L. (1980) Value of wildlife to wilderness users *Proc. 2nd Conf. Sci. Res. in Natl Parks* 6 168–179.

Buckley, R. and Pannell, J. (1990) Environmental impacts of tourism and recreation in National Parks and Conservation Reserves *Journal of Tourism Studies* 1 24–321.

Budowski, G. (1976) Tourism and environmental conservation: conflict, co-existence or symbiosis? *Environmental Conservation* 3(1) 27–31.

Butler, R. (1980) The concept of a tourist area cycle of evolution; implications for management of resources *Canadian Geographer* 24(1) 5–12.

Butler, R.W. (1991) Tourism, environment and sustainable development *Environmental Conservation* 18(3) 201–209.

Cater, E. (1992) Profits from Paradise *Geographical* 54(3) 16–22.

Cater, E. and Lowman, G. (1994) *Ecotourism; A sustainable Option?* Chichester: John Wiley.

Cavalieri, P. and Singer, P. (1993) *The Great Ape Project; Equality Beyond Humanity* London: Fourth Estate.

Cherfas, J. (1984) *Zoo 2000: a look behind the bars* London: BBC.

Christ, C. (1994) Kenya makes revenue sharing top priority *Ecotourism Society Newsletter* 4(1) 1–5.

Cohen, E. (1978) The impact of tourism on the physical environment *Annals of Tourism Research* 5 215–229.

Cole, G.F. (1974) Management involving grizzly bears and humans in Yellowstone National Park *Bioscience* 24(1) 1–11.

Clark, B.D. and Gilad, A. (1989) *Perspectives on Environmental Impact Assessment* Dordrecht: Reidel.

Clark, J.R. (1991) Carrying capacity and tourism in coastal and marine areas *Parks* 2(3) 13–17.

Cook, W.L. (1988) Compatability of tourism and wilderness *Tourism Recreation Research* 13(1) 3–7.

Davies, M. (1990) Wildlife as a tourist attraction *Environment* 20(3) 74–77.

Davis, R.K. (1964) The value of big game hunting in a private forest *Trans. North Am. Wildl. and Nat. Resour. Conf.* 29 393–403.

Decker, D.J. and Goff, G.R. (eds) (1987) *Valuing Wildlife: Economic and social perspectives* London: Westview Press.

de Groot, R.S. (1983) Tourism and conservation in the Galapagos Islands *Biological Conservation* 26 291–300.

Dowling, R. (1991) Tourism and the natural environment: Shark Bay, Western Australia *Tourism Recreation Research* 16(2) 44–48.

Duffus, D.A. and Dearden, P. (1990) Nonconsumptive wildlife-orientated recreation: a conceptual framework *Biological Conservation* 53 213–231.

Eagles, P., Buse, S. and Hvenegaard, G. (1993) *The Ecotourism Society Annotated Bibliography* North Bennington, Vt.: Ecoutourism Society.

Eber, S. (ed.) (1992) Beyond the green horizon. A discussion paper on Princples of Sustainable Tourism, WWF (UK), Godalming.

Economist Intelligence Unit (1991) Managing tourism and the environment – a Kenyan case study *Travel and Tourism Analyst* 2 78–87.

Edington, J. and Edington, A. (1986) *Ecology, Recreation and Tourism* Cambridge: Cambridge University Press.

Eltringham, S.K. (1984) *Wildlife Resources and Economic Development* New York: John Wiley.

Emory, J. (1988) Managing another Galapagos species – man *National Geographic* 173(1) 146–154.

Farrell, B.H. and Runyan, D. (1991) Ecology and tourism *Annals of Tourism Research* 18(1) 26–40.

Fossey, D. (1983) *Gorillas in the Mist* London: Hodder & Stoughton.

Foster, D. (1985) *Travel and tourism management* London: Macmillan.

Frechtling, D.C. (1987) Assessing the impacts of travel and tourism – measuring economic benefits, pp. 333–351 in Richie, J.R.B. and Goeldner, C.R. (eds) *Travel Tourism and Hospitality Research; a Handbook for Managers and Researchers* New York: Wiley.

Getz, D. (1983) Capacity to absorb tourism: concepts and implications for strategic planning *Annals of Tourism Research* 10 239–263.

Gilbert, B. (1976) The great grizzly controversy *Audubon* 78(1) 62–92.

Giongo, F., Bosco-Nizeye, J. and Wallace, G. N. (1994) *A study of visitor management in the World's National Parks and Protected Areas* The Ecotourism Society, Colorado State University, and World Conservation Union, North Bennington, Vt.

Goodall, J. (1986) *The Chimpanzees of Gombe* New York: Balkma/Harvard Press.

Graefe, A.R. and Vaske, J.J. (1987) A framework for managing quality in the tourist experience *Annals of Tourism Research* 14(3) 390–404.

Gunn, C.A. (1988) *Tourism Planning* 2nd edition New York: Taylor and Francis.

Hall, C.M. (1992) Tourism in Antarctica: activities, impacts and management *Journal of Travel Research* 30(4) 2–9.

Hall, C.M. and Weiler, B. (1992) *Special Interest Tourism* London: Belhaven Press.

Harcourt, A.H. (1979–80) Mountain Gorilla Project: progress reports *Oryx* 15 10–11, 114–115, 324–325.

Harcourt, A.H. (1980) Can Uganda's gorillas survive? A survey of the Bwindi Forest Reserve *Biological Conservation* 19 269–282.

Henry, W.R. (1979) Patterns of tourism use in Kenya's Amboseli National Park: implications for planning and management, pp. 43–57 in Hawkins, D.E., Elwood, D., Schafer, J. and Rovestad, M. (eds) *Tourism Marketing and Management Issues* George Washington University, Washington, DC.

Henry, W.R. (1982) Amboseli Park, Kenya: problems of planning and resource management, pp. 34–46 in Singh, T.V. and Kaur, J. (eds) *Studies in Tourism and Wildlife Parks Conservation* Delhi: Metropolitan Book Company.

Herrero, S. (1970) Human injury inflicted by grizzly bears *Science* 170 593–598.

HRSCERA (1989) *Tourism in Antarctica* House of Representatives Standing Committee on Environment, Recreation and the Arts (HRSCERA) Canberra: Australian Government Publishing House.

Hvengaard, G.T., Butler, J.R. and Krystofiak, D.K. (1989) Economic values of birdwatching at Point Pelee National Park, Canada *Wildlife Society Bulletin* 17(4) 526–531.

Ingram, C.D. and Durst, P.B. (1989) Nature-orientated tour operators: travel to developing countries *Journal of Travel Research* 28(2) 11–15.

Inskeep, E. (1991) *Tourism Planning: an integrated and sustainable development approach* New York: Van Nostrand Reinhold.

IUCN (1990) *UN List of National Parks and Protected Areas* IUCN/WCMC, Gland, Switzerland.

Jonkel, C.J. and Servheen, C. (1977) Bears and people: a wilderness management challenge *Western Wildland* Fall 23–25.

Kavanagh, M. and Bennett, E.L. (1984) A synopsis of legislation and the primate trade in habitat and user countries, in Mack, D. and Mittermeier, R.A. (eds) *International Trade in Primates* TRAFFIC (USA).

Kaza, S. (1982) Recreational whalewatching in California, a profile *Whale-watcher* 16(1) 6–8.

Kelly, F.J. (1989) Developing marketing partnerships, pp. 231–242 in *Tourism Research: Globalization of the Pacific Rim and Beyond* Bureau of Economics and Business Research, University of Utah.

Kenchington, R.A. (1989) Tourism in the Galapagos islands: the dilemma of conservation *Environmental Conservation* 16(3) 227–232.

Knetsch, J.L. (1963) Outdoor recreation demands and benefits *Land Economics* 39(4) 387–396.

Krippendorf, J. (1987) Ecological approach to tourism marketing *Tourism Management* 8 174–176.

Laarman, J.G. and Durst, P.B. (1987) Nature travel in the tropics *Journal of Forestry* 85(5) 43–46.

Laarman, J.G. and Perdue, R.R. (1989) Science tourism in Costa Rica *Annals of Tourism Research* 16 205–215.

Lea, J. (1988) *Tourism and development in the Third World* London: Routledge.

Lee, P.C., Thornback, J. and Bennett, E.L. (1988) *Threatened Primates of Africa. The IUCN Red Data Book* IUCN, Gland, Switzerland.

Lillywhite, L. and Lillywhite, M. (1991) Low impact tourism, pp. 162–169 in Hawkins, D.E. and Ritchie, J.R.B. (eds) *World Travel and Tourism Review* Madrid: CAB Publications.

Lindberg, K. (1991) *Policies for maximising nature tourism's ecological and economic benefits* International Conservation Financing Project, Working Paper, World Resources Institute.

Lindberg, K. (1994) Quantifying ecotourism – are reliable statistics in sight? *Ecotourism Society Newsletter* 4(2) 1–3.

Lindberg, K. and Enriquez, J. (1994) *An Analysis of Ecotourism's Economic Contribution to Conservation and Development in Belize* North Bennington, Vt.: Ecotourism Society.

Lindberg, K. and Hawkins, D.E. (1993) *Ecotourism: a Guide for Planners and Managers* North Bennington, Vt.: Ecotourism Society.

Mackinnon, J., Mackinnon, C., Child, D. and Thorsell, J. (1986) *Managing Protected Areas in the Tropics* IUCN, Gland, Switzerland.

McNeeley, J.A. (1988) *Economics and biological diversity: developing and using economic incentives to conserve biological resources* International Union for Conservation of Nature and Natural Resources, Washington, DC: McGregor and Warner.

McNeely, J. and Thorsell, J.W. (1987) *Guidelines for Development of Terrestrial and Marine National Parks for Tourism and Travel* IUCN, Gland, Switzerland.

McNeely, J. and Thorsell, J.W. (1989) Jungles, mountains and islands: how tourism can help conserve the natural heritage *World Leisure and Recreation* 31 29–39.

Markowitz, H. (1982) *Behavioral enrichment in the zoo* Van Nostrand: New York.

Mathieson, A. and Wall, G. (1982) *Tourism: Economic, Physical and Social Impacts* London: Longman.

Mill, R.C. and Morrison, A.M. (1985) *The Tourism System: an introductory text* New York: Prentice-Hall.

Mowforth, M. (1993) *Eco-tourism: terminology and definitions* Research Report Series 1, Dept. of Geographical Sciences, University of Plymouth.

Munn, C.A. (1994) Macaws: winged rainbows *National Geographic* 185(1) 118–140.

Murphy, P.E. (1985) *Tourism: a community approach* London: Routledge.

Myers, N. (1972) National parks in Savannah Africa: ecological requirements of parks must be balanced against socioeconomic constraints in their environment *Science* 178(4067) 1255–1263.

Neil, P.H., Hoffman, R.W. and Gill, R.B. (1975) *Effects of harassment on wild animals – an annotated bibliography of selected references* Special Report 37, 21pp, Colorado Division of Wildlife, Denver.

Norman, R.L., Roper, L.A., Olson, P.D. and Evans, R.L. (1976) *Using wildlife in benefit-cost analysis and mitigation of wildlife losses* Colorado Division of Wildlife, Denver.

Pearce, D.G. (1987) *Tourism Today: a geographical analysis* London: Longman.

Pearce, D.G. (1989) *Tourism development* London: Longman.

Place, S.E. (1988) The impact of national park development on Tortuguero, Costa Rica *Journal of Cultural Geography* 9(1) 37–52.

Place, S.E. (1991) Nature tourism and rural development in Tortuguero *Annals of Tourism Research* 18(2) 186–202.

Plog, S.C. (1974) Why destination areas rise and fall in popularity *Cornell Hotel and Restaurant Administration Quarterly* 15 55–58.

Quesada-Mateo, C.A. and Solis-Rivera, V. (1990) Costa Rica's national strategy for sustainable development *Futures* 22(4) 396–416.

Ream, C.H. (1978) Human-wildlife conflicts in backcountry: possible solutions *Recreational Impacts on Wildlife* Conf. Proc. pp. 153–163.

Robinson, W.L. and Bolen, E.G. (1989) *Wildlife Ecology and Management* New York: Macmillan.

Ryan, C. (1992) *Recreational Tourism* London: Routledge.
Salm, R.V. and Clark, J.R. (1984) *Marine and Coastal Protected Areas: a guide for planners and managers* IUCN, Gland, Switzerland.
Sayer, J.A. (1981) Tourism or conservation in the National Parks of Benin *Parks* 5(4) 13–15.
Schoenfeld, C.A. and Hendee, J.A. (1978) *Wildlife Management In Wilderness* Pacific Grove, Calif.: Boxwood Press.
Shackley, M.L. (1992) Manatees and tourism in southern Florida: opportunity or threat? *Journal of Environmental Management* 34 257–265.
Shackley, M.L. (1993) Guest farms in Namibia: an emerging accommodation sector in Africa's hottest destination *International Journal of Hospitality Management* 12(3) 253–265.
Shackley, M.L. (1995) The future of gorilla tourism in Rwanda *Journal of Sustainable Tourism* 3(2) 1–12.
Shaw, W.W. and Cooper, T. (1980) Managing wildlife in National Parks for human benefits *Proc. 2nd Conf. on Sci. Res. in Natl Parks* 6 189–198.
Shaw, W.W. and Mangun, W.R. (1984) *Nonconsumptive use of wildlife in the United States* Resources Publication 154, US Fish and Wildlife Service, Washington, DC.
Sinclair, M.T. (1992) The tourism industry and foreign exchange leakages in a developing country: the distribution of earnings from safari and beach tourism in Kenya, pp. 185–204 in Sinclair, M.T. and Stabler, M.J. (eds) *The Tourism Industry: an International Analysis* Oxford: CAN International.
Sindiyo, D. and Pertet, F. (1984) Tourism and its impact on wildlife conservation in Kenya *UNEP Industry and the Environment* January–March 14–19.
Smith, C. and Jenner, P. (1989) *Tourism and the Environment* London: Economist Intelligence Unit.
Smith, O.A. Jnr and Giest, A.D. (1965) Comparative psychology in wildlife conservation *American Psychology* 11 1831–1887.
Smith, S.L.J. (1983) *Recreation Geography* London: Longman.
Snepenger, D. (1987) Segmenting the vacation market by novelty-seeking role *Journal of Travel Research* 27(2) 8–14.
Snepenger, D. and Moore, P.A. (1989) Profiling the Arctic tourist *Annals of Tourism Research* 16 566–570.
Sutton, D.B. (1990) From the Taj to the Tiger *Cultural Survival Quarterly* 14(2) 15–19.
Tabata, R. (1989) Implications of special interest tourism for interpretation and resource conservation, pp. 47–59 in Uzzell, D. (ed.) *Heritage Interpretation; Vol 2, The Visitor Experience* London: Belhaven Press.
Tangley, L. (1986) Costa Rica – a test case for the neotropics *Bioscience* 36(5) 296–300.
Theobald, W. (1993) *Global Tourism: The Next Decade* Oxford: Butterworth-Heinemann.
Thompson, R.B. (1977) Effects of human disturbance on an adelie penguin rookery and measures of control, pp. 1177–1180 in Llano, G.A. (ed.) *Adaptation within Antarctic Ecosystems Proc. 3rd SCAR Symp. on Antarctic Biology, 26–30 August 1974* Washington, DC: Smithsonian Institution.

Thresher, P. (1981) The present value of an Amboseli lion *Unasylva* 33(134) 34–35.

Tilt, W.C. (1987) From whaling to whalewatching *Trans. North Am. Wildl. and Natl. Resour. Conf.* 52 567–585.

Vallely, P. (1995) Blood sports meet their Waterloo? *Independent* 3 March 17.

Van Biema, D. (1994) The killing field *Time* 22 August 30–31.

Wace, N. (1990) Antarctica: a new tourist destination *Applied Geography* 10 326–342.

Wallace, G.N. (1993) Visitor management: lessons from Galapagos National Park, pp. 55–68 in Lindberg, K. and Hawkins, D.E. (eds) *Ecotourism: a guide for planners and managers* North Bennington, Vt.: Ecotourism Society.

Weaver, D.B. (1991) Alternatives to mass tourism in Dominica *Annals of Tourism Research* 18(3) 414–432.

Wesley, D.E. (1987) Socio-Duckonomics, pp. 136–142 in Decker, D.J. and Goff, G.R. (eds) *Valuing Wildlife: Economic and social perspectives* London: Westview Press.

Western, D. (1982) Amboseli National Park: human values and the conservation of a savannah ecosystem, pp. 93–100 in McNeely, J.A. and Miller, K.R. (eds) *Proc. World Congr. on National Parks and Protected Areas* Bali, Indonesia.

Western, D. (1986) Tourist capacity in East African Parks *Industry and Environment* 9(1) 14–16.

Western, D. and Henry, W. (1979) Economics and conservation in Third World National Parks *Bioscience* 29(7) 414–418.

Wheeller, B. (1991) Tourism's troubled times: responsible tourism is not the answer *Tourism Management* 12(2) 91–96.

Wight, P. (1993) Ecotourism: ethics or eco-sell? *Journal of Travel Research* 31(3) 3–9.

Witherington, B.W. and Bjorndal, K.A. (1991) Influences of artificial lighting on the seaward orientation of hatchling loggerhead turtles *Caretta caretta* *Biological Conservation* 55(2) 139–149.

World Tourism Organisation (WTO) (1983) *Study of tourism's contribution to protecting the environment* WTO, Madrid.

World Tourism Organisation (1992) *Guidelines: development of National Parks and Protected Areas for tourism* WTO/IUCN Joint Publication, Madrid/Paris.

World Tourism Organisation (1992) *Tourism Carrying Capacity* WTO/UNEP Joint Technical Report Series Tourism, Madrid/Paris.

World Tourism Organisation (1993) *Yearbook of Tourism Statistics* WTO, Madrid.

Yeager, R. and Miller, N.N. (1986) *Wildlife, Wild Death* New York: State University of New York Press.

Ziffer, K.A. (1989) *Ecotourism: the uneasy alliance* Washington, DC: Conservation International and Ernst and Young.

Index

Notes: 1. Page numbers in *italics* indicate illustrations; 2. References to National Parks are ubiquitous and therefore this entry has been omitted from the index